Twayne's United States Authors Series

Edmund Clarence Stedman

TUSAS 286

Edmund Clarence Stedman

EDMUND CLARENCE STEDMAN

By ROBERT J. SCHOLNICK
College of William and Mary

TWAYNE PUBLISHERS
A DIVISION OF G. K. HALL & CO., BOSTON

Library of Congress Cataloging in Publication Data

Scholnick, Robert J
    Edmund Clarence Stedman.

    (Twayne's United States authors series; TUSAS 286)
    Bibliography: p. 175-
    Includes index.
    1. Stedman, Edmund Clarence, 1833-1908—Criticism
and interpretation.
PS2917.S3   811'.4   77-21972
ISBN 0-8057-7188-3

MANUFACTURED IN THE UNITED STATES OF AMERICA

Contents

About the Author

Robert J. Scholnick is Associate Professor of English at the College of William and Mary in Virginia. After graduating from the University of Pennsylvania, he took both advanced degrees at Brandeis University. A specialist in American literature, he has published articles in the scholarly journals on such writers as Whitman, Robinson, Melville, and Bierce.

Preface

This is the first full-length critical study of Edmund Clarence Stedman (1833–1908), poet, critic, literary theorist, anthologist, and, in the words of Harriet Monroe, "the dean of American poets, the friend and helper of young aspirants."[1] Stedman was, as Jay B. Hubbell has observed, "after Lowell and Howells, probably the best critic of American literature in the later nineteenth century," and his lasting contributions to our literature came through his criticism and scholarship, not his poetry.[2] In his major works of practical criticism, *Victorian Poets* (1875) and *Poets of America* (1885), and the theoretical *The Nature and Elements of Poetry* (1892), he persuasively continued Poe's battle against the didactic. He argued for and, in the eleven volume *A Library of American Literature* (1888–1890) actually demonstrated, the reality of an American literary tradition at a time when our writing was thought to be merely an offshoot of English literature. He also brought to criticism the scientific realism of Taine, showing his many readers the importance of seeing the work in its historical and environmental context. But he was also aware of the dangers of a reductive criticism and taught his readers to place biographical and all other secondary considerations in the background so that they might respond to the work itself. In this way, he prepared the way for contemporary practices, particularly our "new criticism." As he wrote in assembling *A Library of American Literature*: "After all, as with the study of Nature, the best way to gain a knowledge of literature is to survey it with our own eyes. Nothing can enable one sooner to test the quality of our native product,—to comprehend its origin and development, and its reflection of the different stages of American history and aspiration,—than such an exhibition as we propose."[3]

A member of the New York Stock Exchange, Stedman spent much of his working life operating his own brokerage firm in New York. This forced him to relegate his literary projects to evenings, weekends, and whatever time he could spare from business. As was not the case with Charles Ives and Wallace Stevens, Stedman's divided life severely limited his personal development and creative achievement. He contained within himself a pervasive American cultural pattern, which George Santayana, in "The Genteel Tradition in American Philosophy," has defined as the absolute divorce in American life between the pragmatic world of business and the ideal world of culture and philosophy. In 1889, Stedman testified to this division when he spoke of poetry as "the chief of the inspired arts—to the natural love and humble study of which all my *better* life has been devoted."[4]

The major purpose of this book is to analyze Stedman's literary achievement. But I have also sought to identify the environmental forces that compelled him to seek fulfillment in both art and business and to trace the resulting pattern of a life that, in its strengths and weaknesses, is characteristically, uniquely, American. The opening chapter is primarily biographical and treats the first forty years of his life—until 1873, when he decided to shift his major literary energies from poetry to criticism. The second chapter studies his first critical volume, *Victorian Poets*, in the context of the postwar interest in developing a systematic and disciplined American criticism. The third chapter shows how, in his next critical work, *Poets of America*, Stedman both attacked the didacticism of the New England heritage and defined a native American tradition. Stedman's response to the idealist-realist controversy is the subject of the following chapter, which pays particular attention to *The Nature and Elements of Poetry*. Succeeding chapters deal with his poetry, his work as editor and anthologist, and his special relationship, during the last twenty-five years of his life, with younger poets.

My interpretations and evaluations of Stedman's work have been done in relation to the standards and views that prevailed in his own time as well as in our own. His judicial essay on Whitman (1880), for instance, becomes more significant when we remember that at the time there was no middle ground between the poet's opponents, who judged him a fraud and charlatan, and his supporters, who treated him as something akin to a saviour. Bypassing the distracting question of personality, Stedman was able to concentrate on Whitman's poetry, and his essay was directly responsible for broad public acceptance of Whitman's genius.

One of the unique strengths of Stedman's own criticism was his use of the historical and environmental perspectives. Citing Taine, he insisted that the critic be aware of the "insensible moulding of an author's life, genius, manner of expression, by the conditions of race, circumstance, and period, in which he is seen to be involved."[5] His evaluations of a writer's achievement were always made with a keen sense of the opportunities available to him. The greatest works, he felt, even while reflecting the contemporary situation, transcend it. Especially in evaluating poetry produced in a hostile and antagonistic period, as he judged his own to be, the critic must be centrally concerned with the dynamic tension between poet and environment. The test of the greatness of the modern artist is his ability to withstand and overcome the destructive forces of his period. Viewed broadly, this is a reasonable criterion to apply to Stedman himself, and I want briefly to outline my conclusions.

Certainly, in what was most important to him—his poetry— Stedman was not able to withstand the debilitating pressures of his divided existence and his "Gilded Age" environment. However, his literary criticism goes far toward overcoming these factors, and it does so in what Santayana, referring to Henry James, called the "classic way, through understanding . . . [by] turning the genteel American tradition. . .into a subject matter for analysis."[6] His scholarly and editorial projects—especially A *Library of American Literature*, the complete edition of Poe, and the famous *An American Anthology*—also contribute to this process of understanding and comprehension by making the national literature available. Finally, in his scrupulous honesty, and especially in his selfless concern for younger writers, Stedman achieved a victory on another level, a human victory not unlike that of James's representative protagonist, Lambert Strether of *The Ambassadors*.

Both Stedman and James's hero were products of a strict, orthodox New England upbringing, and both were limited, in the depth of their commitment to art, by business involvements. But Strether and Stedman persisted in their respective struggles for beauty and self-understanding and toward the end of their lives each managed to share something vital about the nature of the struggle with younger friends.

I should point out here that this approach to Stedman differs in certain important respects from the studies of him through which he is best known, and I have, in turn, formed a new theory to explain one of the major literary conflicts of his time, the "struggle for realism." Willard Thorp has charged Stedman with being the representative theorist of a closely knit band of reactionary writers who, "from the time of the Civil War until past the turn of the century" controlled "the writing and criticism of poetry." This group, which included additionally Thomas Bailey Aldrich, Bayard Taylor, and Richard Henry Stoddard, is alleged to have used its extraordinary influence and power to wage an unyielding battle against "realism," the ordained movement of the future:

The issue was sharply drawn: if one wished to write, one must choose to defend the old order or to throw in one's lot with the new. There was no easy blending of ideality with reality in these uncertain times.

From the time of the Civil War until past the turn of the century, the writing and the criticism of poetry were largely in the hands of a group of friends bound by many personal and literary ties. Presenting a united front to the materialism of the age, resentful of the claims of the realists, they self consciously proclaimed themselves the champions of Ideality in literature. Their influence was so persuasive that when their control over editors and publishers was broken by the writers of the newer generation, the naturalistic revolt was the more violent because they had held it in check for more than a quarter of a century.[7]

But the situation was far more complex than that. On a number of important matters, from judgments regarding individual writers to larger questions of aesthetic philosophy, Stedman in fact advanced positions significantly different from those of other members of the group. The championship of Whitman may serve as a dramatic and obvious example. And he can hardly be charged with using his influence to thwart younger writers. But of more significance than a judgment on this or that writer or issue was Stedman's understanding of the nature of the critical process itself and his use of the scientific realism of Taine, which was not only in advance of other members of his circle but actually contributed to the development of literary realism in this country. The "struggle for realism" was not simply a battle fought between two clearly differentiated and opposed camps, but rather involved conflicts within the minds of individual writers. And in this respect, the critical mind of Edmund Clarence Stedman may be seen as an important battleground for this and other significant literary controversies.

ROBERT J. SCHOLNICK

Williamsburg, Virginia

Acknowledgments

I am grateful to the Faculty Research Committee of the College of William and Mary for grants for the summers of 1970, 71, and 72, which enabled me to undertake this project. Both Mr. Kenneth Lohf, Librarian for Rare Books and Manuscripts at Columbia, and Mr. William F. Bond, Librarian of the Houghton Library at Harvard, have generously allowed me to consult and quote from the Stedman materials in their collections. My colleagues in the English Department at William and Mary have patiently shared with me their knowledge and allowed me to benefit from their criticism. My greatest debt in this, as in everything that I do, is expressed in the dedication of this book to my wife, Sylvia.

Chronology

1833   Edmund Clarence Stedman born in Hartford, Connecticut, October 8.

1835   His father, Edmund Burke Stedman, dies of consumption.

1836   Moves with mother and younger brother to home of maternal grandparents in New Jersey.

1839   Sent to Norwich, Connecticut, to be raised by a greatuncle.

1841   Mother marries William B. Kinney, editor of the Newark *Daily Advertiser*.

1849   Enters Yale in August.

1851   Expelled from Yale for wild behavior.

1852   With a partner, purchases and edits the Norwich *Tribune*.

1853   Dissolves partnership and elopes with Laura Woodworth.

1854   Joins Stephen A. Hubbard in publishing Winstead (Connecticut) *Mountain County Herald*.

1855   Dissolves partnership and moves to New York City, joining the E. A. Ingraham Clock Company.

1856   Becomes real estate and general commission broker. Birth of first child, Frederick Stuart.

1857   Business reverses force him to take a job as clerk for a railroad. Family moves to Unitary Home.

1859   Birth of second son, Arthur, in June. Publishes "Tribune Ballads." Begins friendships with Stoddard, Aldrich, and Taylor.

1860   *Poems, Lyrical and Idyllic*. Joins *Evening World* as day editor.

1861   Becomes *World's* war correspondent. *The Battle of Bull Run*.

1862   Pardon clerk in attorney general's office.

1863   Joins S. Hallett & Co., New York banking firm. *Alice of Monmouth and Other Poems*.

1864   Opens own brokerage firm.

1869   *The Blameless Prince and Other Poems*.

1875   *Victorian Poets*. Physical and mental breakdown forces long Caribbean vacation.

1877   *Hawthorne and Other Poems*.

1883   Discovers that his elder son, Frederick Stuart, has embezzled large sums from firm, forcing a temporary assignment.

1885   *Poets of America*.

1887   "Supplement" added to *Victorian Poets* in the thirteenth edition.

1888–   *A Library of American Literature*, edited with E.M. Hutchin-
1890   son.

1892   *The Nature and Elements of Poetry*.

1894   *The Works of Edgar Allan Poe*, edited with George E. Woodberry.

1895   *A Victorian Anthology*.

1897   *Poems, Now First Collected*.

1899   Serious heart attack in summer.

1900   *An American Anthology*. Retires from business.

1904   Elected one of seven initial members of Academy of Arts and Letters. President through 1907.

1905   Death of wife. Edits *The History of the New York Stock Exchange*.

1906   Death of elder son, Frederick Stuart.

1908   Dies of heart attack on January 19. *The Poems of Edmund Clarence Stedman*.

1910   *Life and Letters*, edited by granddaughter, Laura, and George M. Gould, M.D.

1911   *Genius and Other Essays*.

CHAPTER 1

"Injured for Life"

I A Repressive Childhood

EXPLAINING a reference in *Victorian Poets* to "the barren sentiment of plain New England life," Stedman wrote Thomas Wentworth Higginson, a distant relative, that he had in mind "my personal experience in youth . . . God knows it was plain and barren. It was not the sentiment of Newport or Boston, but of [a] Calvinistic back-country, where I was injured for *life*, and almost perished of repression and atrophy."[1] Stedman was born in Hartford, Connecticut, on October 8, 1833. His father, Major Edmund Burke Stedman, who worked in the family's prosperous lumber business, was thought of popularly as "a downright brave, true gentleman, with a purse open to whoever has need of it, and with never a thought for himself."[2] His sensitive and intelligent mother later achieved a modest critical and popular success for her *Poems* (1867) and verse romances. If the boy had been raised by his parents, it is unlikely that he would have had reason to complain of unusually cruel treatment in childhood. But as a result of his father's death from consumption in December 1835, his grandfathers assumed responsibility for his upbringing, leaving him vulnerable to psychic injury from the forces that he associated with the "Calvinistic back-country."

Edmund Burke Stedman did not leave his widow enough money to maintain her family, and in the spring of 1836 she was forced to sell her furniture and move with her two boys—Charles Frederick had been born the previous August—to the Plainfield, New Jersey, estate of her wealthy father, David Low Dodge (1774–1852).

A staunch Calvinist, Dodge was deeply involved in religious revivals and church affairs. In 1805, after coming close to shooting a man in a case of mistaken identity, he dedicated himself to the cause of universal peace and wrote "the first pamphlets published in America directed expressly against the war system of nations," and

13

established in New York "the first peace society ever organized in America or in the world."[3] Unfortunately for young Ned, as Edmund was called, Dodge's dedication to pacifism did not extend to the upbringing of children or the management of domestic affairs. His daughter wrote that he was "more feared than loved in his family."[4] Stedman recalled that he "taught me to read, and ruled a wild boy according to the old adage of 'Spare the rod, spoil the child!' " (I,5). In fact, his grandfather's beatings, his lessons in "corporeal punishment," were so etched in his memory that as an adult he returned to the large closet where they were administered to relive and relieve his "childhood's terror" (I,14).

Dodge ran an orthodox Calvinist household, insisting upon strict observance of fast days and the Sabbath, days which, one of Stedman's cousins recalled, "seemed very long. . . . After the close of the second service came the long, long afternoon and evening, with no sports, no children's papers, very few books. Our one privilege was to walk slowly down the lane, at the foot of the garden, but not out of it, and then slowly return" (I,13). In this cold, threatening environment, Ned depended upon his mother to provide him with a bastion of love. And, as the following recollection shows, she did respond to the needs of a most unusual child:

> He was a remarkably precocious child from birth, and a very peculiar one. He could read well at four years, and write at six. As soon as he could speak, he lisped in rhyme, and as soon as he could write, he gave shape and measure to his dreams. Often on being put to bed, when he was between five and six, he would get on his knees, bury his head in the pillow, and if told to lie down, and go to sleep, would answer, "Let me alone, please, the *poetry* is coming." (I,15)

"Poetry" very early became a bond between child and mother.

Despite his wealth, Dodge refused to assume financial responsibility for raising his grandsons. Griffin Stedman, Ned's paternal grandfather, offered to support them and even to will them their father's proportional share of his estate, but only if their mother agreed to send the boys to Norwich, Connecticut, to be raised by his brother, James, a lawyer and Latin scholar. Having suffered business reverses, James "raised" boys as a means of supplementing his income. Since James was in debt to Griffin, who doubted that his elderly brother would ever make enough money to repay him, it seemed only logical to charge the regular fees against this debt. The grandfathers found this an ideal business arrangement. Of course, the mother resisted, and tried to earn enough money to support her family by publishing prose and verse in such magazines as *Graham's, Sartain's, Knickerbocker,* and *Godey's Lady's Book.* She learned, however, that an American writer could not then depend upon the magazines for a livelihood— a lesson that her precocious son somehow may have absorbed. Unable, finally, to withstand the pressure of the self-assured male voices around her, she reluctantly gave her consent. In late summer 1839, Ned Stedman, not quite six years old, was dispatched to Norwich.

" 'Tis a bad thing to separate a child from his mother, & from his natural *habitat,*' " Stedman wrote William Rideing in 1887, and behind this simple sentence is the emotional focus of the boy's childhood and adolescence, a painfully insistent desire to be reunited with his mother.[5] As he confessed to her in 1857, "if there has been one longing passion of my heart, since my seventh birthday, above all others, it is that I might live near you and see you often" (I, 128). Nothing in his new life could possibly compensate for his loss. Thomas De Quincy, in "Levana and Our Ladies of Sorrow," an essay that anticipates the insights of modern psychologists into "separation anxiety," has analyzed the plight of boys sent to Eton at six: "Children torn away from mothers and sisters at that age not infrequently die. I speak of what I know. The complaint is not entered by the registrar as grief; but *that* it is. Grief of that sort, and at that age, has killed more than ever have been counted amongst its martyrs."[6] How could a boy of six understand the complex reasons behind the sudden separation? As a first-born son, he felt a powerful need, his letters to his widowed mother show, both to comfort and be comforted by her.[7] As he was allowed only two brief visits a year with her, he found no outlet for these emotions, and they grew to assume ever larger proportions.

During the first year, Ned did not realize that the separation was to be permanent. An active and outgoing child, he quickly involved himself in the exciting world of his uncle's big house, fellow boarders, and Norwich, which he later described as "the quaintest colonial town in New England."[8] The next summer, when he was sent on a trip to Plainfield, he expected at last to be going "home." But after arriving, he realized that he had been sent only to help bring his younger brother back to Norwich. His exile would be permanent. Resisting, he tearfully clung to his mother with all his strength, and could be separated from her only by force.[9]

The next year, the marriage of his mother to William Burnet Kinney (1799–1880), the largest stockholder and editor of the *Newark Daily Advertiser*, complicated his situation. When the newlyweds came to Norwich at Thanksgiving time to visit, both Ned and Charley, as their mother recalled, "begged piteously" to be taken to her new home. But once again Mrs. Kinney acquiesced in the separation:

But Oh! it was hard to part with them again, especially as the eldest, my born poet-baby, rebelled against my leaving him; and never did he become reconciled to our separation. Like all children, both boys were delighted with the idea of having a father . . . and begged piteously to be taken to his home. Had Mr. Kinney seconded their wish, I verily believe that, despite my former consent to the arrangement . . . I should have granted their prayer, though now I had not the legal right to do so. But, to my disappointment Mr. Kinney entirely concurred in the plan of their being brought up by their grandfather Stedman's brother and fitted by him for college. (I, 29)

Over the years he had to watch from afar as his mother and Kinney established a new family. Try as he could to bear it, it hurt him rarely to see his two new half-sisters, to be so totally excluded from the family. "I wish to see Clemmy and Mary very much," he wrote his mother. "It is rather hard for a person not to see his own sisters but once in two or three years. But if I can see them this summer or spring I will not complain" (I, 38). The prospect of a visit to or from his mother was essential to keep up his hope, yet these visits brought with them a special kind of pain: "It was the greatest trial of my life to part from you," he wrote after returning from a visit in April 1848. "I have felt sad & melancholy ever since and I am only reconciled to it by the thought that I shall see you again before long" (I, 39). He hoped to attend Princeton, and so be closer to her. But even here he was to be disappointed; it was decided he would go to Yale.

The wonder is the boy found the emotional toughness to survive at all. Of critical importance to his struggle for independence was his ambiguous relationship with his great-uncle James, whom he recalled as

a fine scholar, noble heart, but also rigid in old-fashioned ways. He taught me Latin, Greek; made me his companion in his law-office, his gardening, his little farm; I daresay loved me more than he showed—as his own sons had not taken to the scholarly studies he still cared for. But we were often at open war. . . . My constant scrapes & rebellion must have tried him beyond measure.[10]

In addition to conveying to Ned a love of scholarship, James provided him with a father figure who cared enough to enter into the sort of conflict through which a boy might forge a resilient toughness.

As the oldest, most adventuresome, and most rebellious of the six boys—three pairs of brothers—who lived with James, Ned Stedman became the leader of the group. He "presented all the petitions to the old gentleman, got credit for all the scrapes, & got most of the thrashings—deservedly, I doubt not, for the others hadn't my imagination, adventurous turn, rebellious independence."[11] According to Margaret Fuller, James, an "exacting and hot-tempered old Puritan," who "did not understand his nephew," was determined to break the boy of his sinful independence. Although "the birch, the spiritual go-between, did its best, . . . it gave out of necessity."[12] James was no match for the strong-willed boy who refused, as he recalled, to "believe in the terrors of the Calvinism about me," especially when that religion was used to impress upon him the depths of his own depravity.[13]

The boy's rich imaginative life made this remarkable strength of will possible. He recalled that his "strongest traits were, first, an inborn & passionate love of beauty—of the beautiful. I was eager to draw, to learn music, etc., & was restricted to my 'studies'; secondly, a love of adventure; third, love of nature & books in equal proportions."[14] Bunyan and Milton he found in his uncle's library, and these he read over so frequently that he supposed "that my style was insensibly affected by their methods and vocabularies" (I, 46). But he did not limit himself to James's library. To borrow secular books, he regularly visited his neighbors. "Of course I got hold of all the great boys' books, of the Robinson Crusoe type; read by stealth the 'Arabian Nights' & 'Fairy Tailes' & believed them."[15] But certainly his mother provided the essential inspiration, as he confessed to her in 1857:

You know that I . . . inheriting my literary tastes from you, turned to books at eight years old as naturally as a child to its mother's breast. I was . . . stimulated by the language and example of yourself, who were the angel of all my young dreams and the rewarder of my ambition. So I went along, *reading everything*,—a heterogeneous mass—till nearly twelve or thirteen years old, at which time I had got along as far as the "Hemans stage" of nonsense. . . . You then gave me a copy of Byron. . . . It was the *wisest thing you ever did*. . . . In a month I was an eloquent votary of the romantic, passionate, subjective "School," of which Byron is unquestionably the English head. . . . For two years I had the *fever* severely, and then slowly began to convalesce. . . . The idea of poetry as an *Art*, began to dawn on me. Soon after I came across Coleridge, Wordsworth, Shelley and Keats. Wordsworth I was not as yet up to, by any means; the more imaginative, or perhaps fanciful, productions of Coleridge, and the whole of Shelley and Keats, were seized upon by me with avidity, and I then merged into an appreciation of the *musical, sensuous* and *artistic*, qualities of poetry. (I, 137–38)

It was after this, Stedman continues, that he discovered Tennyson, who exerted the strongest influence on his style.

II   *Yale*

Terribly anxious to succeed when he enrolled at Yale, Stedman— only fifteen—drew up a list of rules to guide him in fulfilling his religious, academic, and personal responsibilities. In addition to being "present at morning and evening prayers and all other *devotional* exercises" he promised to attend "all *recitations*" and to do so "with my lessons perfectly prepared" (I, 55). Soon he was able to write James that he was "getting on first-rate in my studies and like College right well" (I, 53). But he suffered an emotional shock the next June, when he came to a New York dock to see his mother off on a trip to Italy. Mr. Kinney had been appointed *chargé* to the court of Sardinia at Turin, where, according to the *DAB*, he did a splendid job.[16] But Mrs. Kinney vividly recalls the sadness of

my poet-boy! with his wistful eyes fastened on me so that it seemed as if nothing *could* tear him from the mother he worshipped afar off for the last sad years. He grew so tenacious in his looks, and in the pressure of the hand which held mine, that I began to fear he would not let go. . . . But when . . . we sailed . . . I . . . discovered Edmund [on the dock] holding on to a beam for support, his face pale, and his eyes peering out through their tears to catch the last farewell-glance that mine left behind. Oh, what a moment was that! His earnest, almost despairing look was photographed on my heart, and time has never effaced it. (I, 56–57)

The ambitious Stedman was able to win the sophomore prize in English composition, for which, instead of the usual prose, he submitted a long, elaborately inscribed poem, "Westminister Abbey." Yet, as he wrote in 1871, without "a single friend or advisor in New Haven . . . from utter loneliness, trouble, and inexperience, I fell into the dissipation that drew me from my proper studies" (I, 453).

He read Poe and Landor, associated with a wild crowd, ignored regular studies, and spent his nights "howling around town."

Arrested one night, he was rusticated to a school in Northampton. There he joined "a still wilder crowd . . . in painting the town red, getting in love with the Northampton girls and into trouble generally" (I,72). In December, Stedman and some friends traveled to Springfield to stage a "Series of Dramatic Rehersals" of Shakespearean scenes—a performance that previews the Royal Nonesuch of *Huckleberry Finn*. The handbill informed the citizens that the actors, "THE WELL KNOWN TRAGEDIAN, ALFRED WILLOUGHBY, and his sister, MISS AGNES WILLOUGHBY, . . . have returned from their professional tour in Europe, where they have fulfilled engagements in all the PROVINCIAL THEATRES of note." The slight, boyish Stedman was Agnes, whose "delicate health" required that the actors soon "quit the stage." Poor attendance the first evening led them to reduce ticket prices, but as reported in the press, "before evening came, they took the cars for the North. . . . The great question in Springfield now is—'who are Mr. and Miss Willoughby?' " (I,78–79). The Yale authorities had no trouble with the problem and promptly expelled Miss Agnes.

After a trip South—while in New York, Horace Greeley assured him there were no vacancies on the *Tribune*—a chastened and repentent young man returned to Norwich, now determined to atone for his transgressions by living responsibly in the adult world. Twenty years later, in his successful petition to have Yale award him the B.A. and M.A., he wrote President Woolsey, who had expelled him,

As soon as I realized my error, I resolved to obtain a higher culture, and to accomplish something that would gain me an honorable name and position. Since my eighteenth year I have studied and worked, dependent entirely upon my own efforts, and with others depending upon me; and believe that I may claim to have secured a reputable and useful foothold, both as a practical journalist, and as a critical essayist and author. (I,453)

This rebellion served, ironically, as Stedman's rite of passage into adulthood.

After reading law with James for several months, Stedman, in partnership with Charles B. Platt, purchased a fledgling weekly, the Norwich *Tribune*, and the associated printing plant. Stedman edited the paper; Platt ran the job printing business. Discovering that they were both in love with the same girl, Laura Woodworth, then working as a seamstress, the chivalrous young partners, not willing to have their friendship destroyed by romantic rivalry, agreed to send her identical copies of a letter explaining the situation and politely requesting her to choose between them—if she could love either. In winning the competition, Stedman also assumed significant financial responsibilities: he immediately arranged for Laura to leave the sewing room and board in a private household where she could prepare for an educational institution. Stedman's financial situation was complicated by the failure of the *Tribune* to make headway against two established rivals. In June 1853 the paper closed, Stedman selling his share of the profitable job printing business to Platt. In November, partially as an act of defiance against both James, who insisted that his unpredictable nephew live quietly at home until he reached his majority, and the "important world of Norwich," which doubted the sincerity of his attentions to a poor seamstress, Ned and Laura eloped. Early the next year, they went to Winstead, Connecticut, where Stedman joined with Stephen Hubbard in publishing the *Mountain County Herald*.

Stedman was fortunate in his choice of a mate. After a few months of marriage, he "began to see that what I had done partly from caprice—partly from sympathy—partly from rivalry—most of all from pride—was a *good* thing for myself; that I had secured a true, loving heart and a nature as quiet and unostentatious, as it was devoted, for my own. I began to love her, and have loved her more and more ever since" (I,101). The marriage was not broken until Laura's death in 1905.

All this time Stedman expected that he would inherit his father's share of Griffin Stedman's estate on his twenty-first birthday in 1854. But when he came of age, he learned that he and Charley had been cut from the will. Henceforth, he could depend only upon his own resources. Now his responsibilities as husband must take precedence over the claims of the poetic career that both he and his mother had always assumed would be his. Convinced for most of his early manhood that he would follow his father to a consumptive's early grave, he keenly felt the necessity of building an estate for his family. Especially after the birth of his children, Fred in 1856 and Arthur in 1859, he could not bear the possibility of leaving a young widow and two infant sons to the mercies of the world, as his father had done. Still, his deepest ambitions were literary, and he refused to give up hopes of a literary career.

III   *Golden New York*

Initially, journalism offered the logical way to resolve these conflicts. He and Laura enjoyed life in Winstead. Shortly after his arrival, he wrote proudly to James that "I have awoke, as it were, and found myself in control of a large and driving business, without much extraordinary effort to get there, and certainly with no pecuniary aid. And as I am yet very young, I hope with prudence and energy to make my 'pile' " (I, 105). Under his direction, the paper was recognized for its reasoned approach to politics and "correct literary tone."[17] But as was to be the case throughout his life, Stedman, when succeeding in one area, felt guilty about neglecting the other. In October 1854 he published the Tennysonian "Amavi" in the prestigious *Putnam's Monthly*.[18] The lure of New York was irresistible. In April 1855 he sold his share of the business, and shortly thereafter moved to the metropolis, explaining to his mother,

I did *not* like the reputation of being 'E. C. Stedman, Esq. the talented young editor of the *Bungtown Gazette*'—a reputation fast spreading. The man who has the reputation of a *good second rate actor* can never touch the Audience like a 'Star' even if he plays *as well*. *Aut Caesar—aut nihil*. And so I found that money-grabbing was the principal part of country editing, and not a moment's time for heavy writing. I thought I might as well be at something that would give me a little time to write for myself, study, etc., and so came to New York—to do *business* eight hours a day, I thought, instead of twelve, and have my evenings to cultivate higher 'literary associations' than editing a country paper never so well could procure for me. (I, 109)

He managed the New York store of A. Ingraham & Company, the famous Connecticut clock firm, in which he purchased an interest.

After a disastrous warehouse fire, Stedman left the clock business to become a real estate and general commission broker, an experience that exacerbated his dislike of business in general. "It is everywhere diamond cut diamond—profit piled on profit—till at last the poor *consumer* pays twice what a thing is worth, and all to fatten the crowd of unnecessary middle men" (I, 118). But he responded not with outrage, but with a guilty acceptance:

I growl at business, because I have a *right* to—being now business man and doing as well as any of them, at their dirty, sordid, but alas! alas! alas!—sadly necessary pursuit. But . . . I feel like Moses in the wilderness, and think perhaps I have a mission, and shall get at it one of these days. . . . "I see a hand they cannot see, which beckons me away!" So while I am at business, I will do just as others do, whom I see making money, and generally esteemed, and if I can bring any genius to bear, and do it more quickly and genteely than others, why, so much the better, and then good-bye to it forever. (II, 535–36)

Only at the end of his career did Stedman come to take pride in practicing a profession that did, in fact, serve a necessary economic function in his society, one in which most members—with some notorious exceptions—did fulfill the demands of a code that assumed individual integrity. Now, however, perhaps reflecting the religious training of his childhood, he could not help but perceive the problem of occupation in starkly moral terms: the evil of commerce stood in conflict with the high purity of art. Forced to give himself up into the hands of the devil, he restored to a fancy mental trick; like Moses, he had heard a "voice" and would be saved. He was unprepared, then, to face realistically the harmful side effects of practicing a profession that an important part of him hated.

The brokerage business is inherently unstable, and financially 1858 was disasterous for Stedman. He was forced to accept a minor position in the office of a railroad and even to sell his home. With capital rapidly disappearing, the family moved to Edward Underhill's Unitary Home, a commune founded on the principles of Fourier. The move, as Stedman recalled, partly reflected a continuing "Revolt against the methods and environment of my exile in Norwich." Further, he "had read a good deal of Fourier," and like many in the prewar years, was anxious to commit himself to a utopian scheme (I, 153). But mundane considerations were also involved; Stedman was dispirited by his business failures and his inability to form literary friendships. The Home proved to be a great bargain; nowhere else could such excellent lodgings and food be obtained for the minimal charges that communal practices made possible. And, for the first time since coming to New York, Stedman regularly associated with creative individuals, many of them newspapermen.

Underhill, for instance, had an editorial position on the *Tribune*, as did the brilliant and fiery Charles Taber Congdon. Alfred C. Hill worked as city editor of the *Evening Post*. Inhabiting the upper reaches of the house, Stedman recalled, were the "Slaves of the Lamp"

free-lances, news gatherers, or when items fell short, *making news*, and selling it as best they could. In those days, outside the editorial page, the foreman of the *Herald* office slapped in what he chose. There was plenty of space for full reports of speeches at political meetings, and Cooper Institute . . . was temptingly near for our behemian free-lances to take down the 'outside speeches,' on the chance of selling column matter to one of the newspapers. One evening I remember that a couple of our boys had obtained the news of the credited orators, but failed to 'take' their outgivings, whereupon Hill and [Leonard A.] Hendricks [of the *Herald*] mounted boxes in the former's room, as spell-men, and improvised enough eloquence to fill a couple of columns, which greatly to the surprise of my ingenuous mind, was sold to the *Herald*, and appeared therein a few hours afterwards, doubtless, much to the perplexity of the orators purporting to have delivered it. (I,169)

The key to survival in the competitive world of free-form journalism was to find or invent a story related to some topic of strong current interest and then report it in a lively way. Stedman soon proved his ability to do this in verse.

In the fall of 1859, the press gave ever-increasing attention to the extravagant courtship of the reigning New York beauty, a teenage girl of limited means, by an elderly and wealthy Cuban planter. New York had its first taste of what, following the war, would become only too familiar, elaborate reports, as Stedman described it, of "a champagne aristocracy composed of the families of parvenu contractors, speculators successful in the Stock Market and the Gold Room, whose opera boxes, yachts, trotters, and clothes, were for all the world to see" (I,184). The day after the opulent wedding, Stedman dashed off a satiric ballad, "The Golden Wedding." In recounting the story, the poem laments the decline of established virtues in the corrupt, materialistic age of publicity: "But now, True Love, you're growing old—/Bought and sold, with silver and gold,/Like a house, or a horse and carriage!"[19]

Published on October 18 in the *Daily Tribune* and extensively reprinted, "The Golden Wedding" surprised the author by creating an immediate sensation. The bride's father challenged Stedman to a duel and threatened him with a lawsuit. Guided by the sage advice of his Unitary Home colleagues, Stedman dexterously parried these thrusts, winning for himself an even greater notoriety.

As society verse, the poem is artistically successful. Further, it helped prick a ridiculous bubble, and such satire was especially needed in the unsettled prewar years. The aggressive young publisher G. W. Carleton urged Stedman to allow him to print the poem in a format similar to that devised for William Allen Butler's *Nothing to Wear*. With drawings by Augustus Hoppin and priced at fifty cents, this "pamphlet poem" had a huge sale, "even in the panic year of 1857."[20] But Stedman, as he explained to his mother, hesitated, "because I consider satire a poetic heresy, and don't wish any reputation as the author of stuff like this, of which either you or I could write a cart-load '*stans pede in uno*,' but if I consent they will pay handsomely, and I am so poor this Fall I cannot buy Winter clothes for my Family" (I,197). In a decision that he later termed "priggish," he refused to allow Carleton to publish it. Looking back, he tried to suggest some of the humor of his situation: "Were those lyrics and idyls which I had been writing, keyed to the note, and reminiscent of Wordsworth, Shelley, Keats, and above all, Tennyson, my master who had drawn the best from all, and of whom I knew I was one of the few adherents, worshipping him afar off—were the joy and fame of these pieces, in the realms of high art, to be subordinate to the mere notoriety so strikingly aroused by the production of a newspaper skit, so easy for me to write, and so utterly out of my desire?" (I,188). Ironically, his very commitment to "high art" kept him from developing the limited, but real, poetic talent he did have, for light or society verse.

The *Tribune* did not pay Stedman for "The Golden Wedding" or the two other popular ballads that it published, "How Old Brown Took Harper's Ferry" and "The Ballad of Lager Bier," but he was given a staff job early in 1860. He soon found the reportorial and editorial "hack work" that he was called upon to perform distasteful. After filing a long account of a sensational execution in New Jersey, he noted in his diary, "Shameful to earn a living in this way" (I,215). Like most contemporary journalists, he was woefully underpaid. To make ends meet, he had to write letters on New York social life for the Chicago *Press* and *Tribune* and place "features" wherever he could. But as a skilled journalist, Stedman made rapid progress. In July, he was appointed editor of the paper's weekly edition, and in August he joined Manton Marble's *Evening World* as day editor. A paper with religious antecedents, the *Evening World* had been dubbed "The Night-blooming Serious" by Henry Clapp's irreverent *Saturday Press*.[21] Stedman's wealthy New York uncle, William E. Dodge (who built Phelps Dodge & Co. into one of the country's leading metals firms), purchased stock in the paper for him so that, in the nephew's words, he might have "a proper status in the concern" (I,228).

In the offices of the *Tribune* he met Bayard Taylor and through him Richard Henry Stoddard, the New York poets whose work meant the most to him. Reacting against the didacticism of Longfellow, these New Yorkers placed new emphasis on the beauty of poetic statement. In 1885 Stedman recalled that certain of the individual poems of Stoddard's *Songs of Summer* (1855) were "among the first to initiate the movement here in *poetry for poetry's sake*. It set in from the time R. H. S., B. T., and a few others began to write" (II,92). At Stoddard's urging, Stedman assembled his first collection, *Poems, Lyrical and*

Idyllic, which Charles P. Scribner, on Stoddard's recommendation, published in April of 1860. *Harper's Monthly* described the verses as "productions of a mind naturally attuned to the expression of melody, but one not yet fully master of its own powers of reflection or illustration. Several of the descriptive poems are of unusual excellence; most of the volume betrays a genuine gift of song, and indicates the promise of a brilliant future."[22] A warm friendship between the three couples, the Stedmans, Stoddards, and Taylors, quickly developed. The Taylors and the Stoddards were then sharing living quarters, on Thirteenth Street, and when Stedman sent his family to the New Jersey countryside for the summer, he took a bachelor's room with them.

Stedman and Laura regularly attended the "Saturday Evenings" given by the Taylors and Stoddards. Regular guests included such figures as Edwin Booth, N. P. Willis, R. W. Griswold, and Albert Bierstadt. Most were married. The poets among them, as Stedman later wrote of Stoddard, had "found that the literary market of that time gave returns that needed supplementing by another means of support."[23] Stoddard held a custom house appointment; Taylor was a star journalist, travel writer, and lecturer; and Aldrich, while not yet as firmly settled as he would be after moving to Boston, had been in business and had assisted Willis in editing the *Home Journal* from 1856 to 1859. While not exactly conventional, the society was composed of individuals who had made their peace with the social order.

Mrs. Thomas Bailey Aldrich recalled that the Stoddard's home served as one of the "three literary centres in New York at this time."[24] The Bohemians, whose central figure was Henry Clapp, regularly met at Pfaff's cellar restaurant, where Walt Whitman held forth. At the other extreme was the forbidding Century Club, then out of reach of a young newspaperman like Stedman. Since literary New York was comparatively small and most of the younger writers knew one another, the lines between the two groups were not strictly drawn. Stedman visited Pfaff's occasionally and considered such Bohemians as George Arnold, "Ada Clare," Clapp, Fitz-James O'Brien, and Frank Wood to be his friends. But Stedman refused to be identified with them. Similarly, Howells, who formed his "first impressions of literary New York at this time," "liked the Stoddards because they were frankly not of that Bohemia which I disliked so much, and thought it of no promise or validity; and because I was fond of their poetry and fond of them."[25] Stedman himself was involved in

some of the conflict between the two groups. Following the great
popular success of his satire "The Prince's Ball" in *Vanity Fair*, a
magazine associated with the Bohemians, Stedman wrote his mother,
"all the old Bohemian crowd, my assailants, are making friends again"
(I, 219). Ironically, Stedman did allow Rudd and Carleton to bring out
this forced poem in pamphlet form; it is clearly inferior to "The
Golden Wedding."

The differing expectations of the two groups regarding the artist's
social position was one source of conflict. In 1890 Stedman blamed
the tragically high mortality rate among the Bohemians during these
years on the

pace, the hard work, the irregular income. . . .
     There was not much of a literary market at that time. Newspaper salaries
were very low. There were few magazines, and scarcely any but *Harper's* and
the *Atlantic* paid much of anything. New York itself was not literary and
looked with distrust, if not contempt, upon working writers. These people
were mostly from the country. They had scarcely any acquaintances in the
city outside of their profession. You can easily see that they were thrown back
upon themselves and made the most of that artistic, happy-go-lucky
bonhomie and comradeship. (I, 209)

In later life he would justify his business career by pointing to the
unacceptable risks of the Bohemian garret for a family man. But this
was really a false issue, one which may have served to keep him from
admitting his monetary and social ambitions. And the demands of his
business career provided a convenient excuse for his artistic failures.
As he pointed out with regard to Bayard Taylor, "Men do not escape
from tasks they once assume, and he had undertaken to earn a large
income and survey the world, on the one hand, and to hold the Muse
by her pinions on the other. His poetry had to be composed 'between
spells,' and on the wing."[26]

But while he was alive, Taylor, through the force of his
extraordinary personality and his established position as poet,
novelist, diplomatist, translator, scholar, lecturer, travel writer, and
newspaperman, seemed to prove just the opposite: that the poet
could achieve social prominence, make and spend money, and serve
his art at the same time. Just now he was completing his magnificent
country estate, Cedarcroft, in rural Pennsylvania. And over the next
fifteen years he became Stedman's most trusted literary friend and
most important correspondent. Each found the encouragement and
reassurance of the other helpful in sustaining a life of "divided

ambition." "Let us be cheery," Stedman wrote Taylor on Christmas 1873, "and trust to gain and hold a steadily surer footing. We can hold one another's hands, at all events!" (I,491). The following excerpt from Stedman's last letter to Taylor—then mortally ill—may serve to define the older man's crucial importance not only to Stedman, but to others of the "circle:"

Nothing but the absolute sense of my wish & duty to stand by you conquers my sense of inability so to do, or to do anything *rightly* where my *heart* is involved. Light emotions make me easily loquacious, as you know; but at those times when I feel the most, & ought to do the most, I often can say nothing & do nothing—like a man in the crisis of a dream.—So much trouble, so much awry, of late, everywhere,—in our own affairs—in the circle of the few whom we love—that it seems as if the world, for us, were disintegrating, and we grow mute and rigid.

Well: I know your inherent, inherited vitality; your splendid mould & courage, your buoyant hope. You are not like the common sort, and I am *sure* you are going to conquer your physical assailants . . . and bring back life & hope to the entire group of which you are the central figure.[27]

But it was only after Taylor's death that Stedman's life as a critic of American literature began. And then he had first to come to grips with Taylor's limitations.

IV *A Poet's War*

The eagerness with which Stedman responded to the Civil War gives some indication of his underlying dissatisfaction with his New York life. Even before the outcome of the battle at Fort Sumpter was known, he urged, in a *World* poem, "Sumpter," that the country undertake the most vigorous possible warfare to punish the unforgivable "sin" of the South in attacking the "hallowed State."[28] He immediately went to Washington as the *World's* war correspondent and was soon out in the field with the troops. Campaigning delighted him. "We had a perfectly magnificent time to-day," he wrote Laura. "I never enjoyed a day so much in my life. Was in the van throughout, at the head of the army, and it was exciting and dramatic beyond measure" (I,230). He recognized that in part his support of the war was selfish: it supplied his need for "personal shaking-up and *rejuvenating*—the old *healthy* love of *action* rising in me" (I,241).

The outbreak of war transformed Stedman into a believer in the divinely sanctioned state. He admitted in a long letter to his mother in October 1861 that "for eight years I have cared *nothing* for politics—have been disgusted with American life and doings." But now he could be "proud of my country and my grand, heroic brethren. The greatness of the crisis, the Homeric grandeur of the contest, surrounds and elevates us all." (I,242). This letter is particularly valuable because it explains why so many Northerners who were not abolitionists fervently supported the Union cause. Later in the war, Stedman would call himself an "abolitionist, so far as hatred of slavery is concerned," (I,284) but now he insists that the war "is *not* the result of abolitionism. We are not sure but that slavery is a very good thing in the Cotton states. In other latitudes I see for myself that it is good enough for the negroes, but ruinous to the whites." The "real cause . . . is a bitter and criminal hatred, entertained by the South against the North." Controlling the national government, the South has "lorded it" over the North, and now is unwilling to abide by the results of a fair election (I,242,243). Unless the North punishes the South, it will lose all self-respect. Beyond this, Stedman expected that in the very process of defeating the South, the Union would be transformed into a leading world power (I, 240–47).

He seriously considered entering military service himself, but reported to his mother that he finally rejected, "on your account and Laura's, offers of Colonel's and Major's commissions for the War" (I,246). However, as a war correspondent, he sometimes took an active part in fighting the battles he covered. The high point of his Civil War campaigning was the first Bull Run battle. The Philadel-phia *Inquirer* reported that as the panic-stricken retreat of the Union troops developed, Stedman retrieved the fallen standard of the Massachusetts Fifth and "succeeded in rallying a large force" (I,235). His masterful account of the battle for the *World*, "often cited as one of the most graphic of battle dispatches," sold thousands of copies in the news-starved North when reprinted in pamphlet form by Rudd and Carelton.[29] But by January 1862 he had managed to secure a most attractive government position, as pardon clerk in the office of Attorney General Edward Bates. His responsibilities were hardly burdensome, and Bates, who liked Stedman, regularly gave him permission to cover important battles for the *World*, enabling him to double his annual salary of $1,550. This marked the first step in his withdrawal from the conflict he had welcomed so enthusiastically.

In the early spring of 1862 he was probably the most prominent reporter to be "used" by General George B. McClellan in his bid for "badly needed editorial support." McClellan and members of his staff fed him "news leaks," and in turn Stedman brought the *World* to support McClellan editorially.[30] However, after the failure of McClellan's Peninsula campaign—during which Stedman was almost killed by a sniper near Williamsburg—he lost confidence in McClellan. His poem "Wanted—A Man," which appeared in the *Daily Tribune* on September 9, 1862, "spoke for the whole North," as one historian has noted, in calling for new military leadership, for "a Hero" to lead "the Holy War!—/Abraham Lincoln, give us a MAN!"[31] Later that fall, Stedman resigned from the *World* after it came out for the Copperhead position. This involved a real financial sacrifice, as he wrote to Taylor: "lost all my stocks, & a handsome salary. Any *man* had rather starve than consort with the Wood-Seymour-Belmont clique."[32] He attacked this "clique" in another influential war poem, "Treason's Last Device," published in the *Tribune* for January 24, 1863.

But as the war ground on, with little apparent progress and unparalleled suffering, death, and destruction, it could no longer be seen as a "grand Homeric" spectacle. Early in 1863 Stedman recognized that this war challenged each citizen in a radically new way, as he explained to the Stoddards:

Who, indeed, amongst the suffering and devotion here present, can be so base as to think of self. The humanities here developed by lowly men are grand and worshipful, whether wasted in a mismanaged cause or destined to win it finally. So Walt Whitman seems to think; he is in town, and for a month has devoted himself to the hospitals. I don't know him, though he passes me daily; but I guess he has a good heart and is a noble fellow, despite his erratics. (I, 308–09)

From Whitman's radically democratic perspective, each citizen must freely subordinate his individual interest to the larger cause; the powerful should learn from the magnificent humanity of the average man. Stedman expressed a similar idea in a poor *Round Table* poem that he never reprinted, "Robes of Honor." Here he attacks the "Newly rich," whose "Fresh-gilt fortunes . . . have grown/While heroes fall and captives moan."[33]

But no more than the country as a whole was Stedman able to respond adequately to such a moral imperative. In March 1863, he wrote his brother of his discouragement at not being "*established* in life. All my cousins, my classmates, are either laying up something, or are rich, or in high political or military places, and are sure of the future" (I,314). In August 1863, influenced more by the spectacle of the powerful enriching themselves than by the sacrifices of the common man, Stedman accepted a year's contract with the banking firm of Samuel Hallett, at a salary of $2,500. In October, Whitman wrote his brother Jeff of "a fellow, E. C. Stedman, [who] has been here till lately, is now in Wall Street, he is poor but he is in with the big bankers . . . who are in with [General John Charles] Fremont in *his* line of Pacific railroad." Walt offered to give Jeff a letter of introduction if he were interested in obtaining a job through Stedman.[34] Finally, Stedman became yet another writer of his generation who withdrew from the Civil War. His melodramatic long poem, "Alice of Monmouth: An Idyl of the Great War" (1863), portrays the war more as a glorious combat of heroic knights than as the first modern war it was. He used the war as a dramatic backdrop for the sad, yet ennobling, love affair of a spotless hero and his beautiful lady. James Russell Lowell concluded his enthusiastic *North American* notice by observing, "we have found it hard to criticise at all a poem which brought warm tears to our eyes more than once as we read."[35] But, to use Whitman's phrase, it certainly was not "the real war" that Stedman put into his book.

V *Wall Street*

Stedman served Hallett as a sort of high-class public relations man. He edited the *American Circular*, a paper promoting the interests of the railroad, and frequently traveled to Washington to see government officials, including Salmon P. Chase, the secretary of the treasury, on behalf of his firm's clients. At the beginning of 1864, he took a leave of absence from the firm to work as an organizer of the abortive campaign to nominate Chase for the presidency on the Republican ticket in place of Lincoln. He also found time to speculate in the stock market for his own account. His extraordinary success in this enabled him to purchase a "dream house" in April. In the midst of all of this activity, he still found time to write reviews for the *Round Table* and to resume his literary friendships. That fall, after Hallett's murder, Stedman opened a successful brokerage firm of his own. In December he could look back on a year which "has been pecuniarily my best one yet. It opened on me very poor. Am now in our own home, and with some little means. Am grateful that my dear ones will not be wholly *dependent*, if I should suddenly die. And if I am to live a little longer, I *may* be able to resume my art and studies" (I, 349).

At the beginning of 1865, Stedman's goal of financial independence was quite within reach. His speculations, as far as I have been able to determine, had netted him at least $10,000, and he possessed a thriving brokerage business. A few more years of such prosperity would have brought him enough capital to subsidize a writing career. But he lacked the emotional stability to persevere. His original business objective had been to devote virtually all of his energy to his own speculations and to limit strictly the number of outside commissions he would accept. Foolishly, he allowed the commission business to grow so rapidly that he could not control it, and had to take in one partner after another, each time surrendering a portion of the firm. Finally, in the spring, with his health deteriorating, he sold his "last interest in the concern for a trifle, to save my life" (I,355).

To recover, Stedman and Laura visited the Taylors at Cedarcroft, and then spent the remainder of the summer camping in the Adirondack wilderness. Here he enjoyed his favorite sport, trout fishing, and came increasingly to understand Thoreau's "entire satisfaction with wild-life" (I,364). At last, he was able to overcome the fear that he faced a consumptive's premature death. Back home in New York in the fall, he felt himself restored:

I have been leading my beau-ideal life . . . *writing from breakfast to lunch* in my library; lunch at home; then down town leisurely for exercise and business. To be sure, I am getting as poor as Poverty, but the Lord never intended that I should, at any one time, have health and money both. You cannot imagine with what zest I have gone back to my books! I did not know there was so much of the old love left in me. It seems as if I never wanted to leave my library, and as if my business life were a dream. (I, 369).

Now he began an ambitious project, one which he would never finish, a complete translation of the Syracusan poets—Theocritus, Bion, and Moschus—into English hexameters. After spending a morning immersed in classical scholarship, he must have felt, during his afternoon strolls, much like "Pan in Wall Street," to use the title of the characteristic poem written at this time. In the midst of the "sordid city," near "the Treasury's marble front," a musician, Pan himself, appeared and the narrator

heard a strange, wild strain
Sound high above the modern clamor,
Above the cries of greed and gain,
The curbstone war, the auction's hammer;
And swift, on Music's misty ways,
It led, from all this strife for millions,
To ancient, sweet-do-nothing days
Among the kirtle-robed Sicilians.[36]

In Stedman's case the policeman who "scoffed the vagrant demigod, / And pushed him from the step I sat on," thereby ending the pleasing music, was economic necessity, which forced him to reopen his business in October 1866.

But the interval was productive. Stedman published prose and verse in the prestigious Boston magazines, the *Atlantic* and *North American*, as well as in such new local periodicals as the *Round Table, Nation*, and the *Galaxy*. Taylor, who helped him establish the connection with the *Atlantic*, congratulated him jocularly on it: "Rejoice my friend! Boston hath accepted you!" But such was the prestige of the journal that Taylor had to comment, "in all gravity, this is a good thing, because the 'Atlantic' is accepted by the populace as the representative magazine of American literature, and your name there secures you the respect of all the small fry."[37]

While of course respecting the *Atlantic's* prestige, Stedman came to resent what he perceived as its high-handed treatment of non–New England writers. Accordingly, he actively supported the *Galaxy*, a monthly that had been founded early in 1866 by his friend Colonel William C. Church with his brother, Francis P. Church, as a cosmopolitan rival to the sectional *Atlantic*. "The Churches are doing their bravest to establish a *N. Y. mag.* & ought to be helped & encouraged by N. Y. authors," he wrote Taylor in May.[38] Although the *Round Table* was forced to suspend permanently in July 1869, the victim of its weekly rival, the *Nation*, and the *Galaxy*, ironically, was absorbed by the *Atlantic* in 1878, the founding of these magazines presaged the gradual emergence in the postwar decades of New York as the country's literary center. In December 1873, following James Osgood's sale of the declining *Atlantic* to Henry Houghton, Stedman wrote Taylor that it had been one of his long-held "theories" "that the sceptre would come back from Boston to N. Y., after a time." Several years earlier he had "cut loose (mostly) from the *Atlantic*, and have thrown all my advice, influence, work, in favor of the 'coming monthly,' [New York-based] *Scribner's*" (I, 489). Of particular significance for Stedman's development as a writer, the emergence of New York coincided with increasing recognition of the importance of literary criticism. As he observed in the preface to *Victorian Poets*, "Criticism, like science, latterly has found a more interested public than of old."[39] Writers found in New York a broad, diversified, and paying market for criticism. In responding to this market, Stedman discovered his interest in and talent for criticism, and developed his critical theory and technique.

He contributed a theoretical essay, "Elements of the Art of Poetry," to the *Galaxy* for July 1866 and in the same month, "English Poetry of the Period," appeared in the *North American.* One of the New York journals, most likely the *Round Table,* asked him to review R. H. Stoddard's anthology, *The Late English Poets.* But in offering the article to Lowell instead, he explained that "I have insensibly expanded its proportions and cared for its style, until it seems not only too long, but too good, for the journal in question" (I,369). At the time, *Scribner's* had not been founded and the *Galaxy* had yet to appear. There was no suitable New York journal. He explained to Lowell that his essay compares the contemporary situation in English poetry with the Alexandrian age, "when the poets of the day resorted to all sorts of quaint, involved, spasmodic devices, to cover defective creative faculty, but when criticism, philology, and general learning, were widely mastered" (I,370). *Victorian Poets* is a development of this idea.

Lowell took a personal interest in Stedman, visiting him in New York and sending him frank letters full of literary opinions and advice. The younger man told Lowell that his "advice and friendship are naturally more to one of my habits than could be those of any other American" (I,376). Indeed, such was the impact of Lowell's letters, that Stedman "often found himself repeating sentences from them" (I,372). Lowell urged Stedman to complete the Theocritus translation and to do it in hexameters, criticized him for writing a "naughty" poem, "Anonyma—" (the monologue of a prostitute), cautioned him against negative criticism of contemporary authors ("If I don't like a thing and there's otherwise no harm in it, I hold my tongue."), and condemned the "Adamite" heresy of Swinburne's *Laus Veneris.*[40] As strong as Lowell's influence at this time became, surely Howard Mumford Jones is right in denying John Paul Pritchard's claim that Stedman was simply one of Lowell's "Epigoni."[41] We will see, for instance, how angry Lowell became when Stedman did not "hold his tongue" and exposed the limitations of his work in *Poets of America.* Stedman vigorously championed Swinburne and Rossetti, whom Lowell had attacked. Finally, Stedman's Tainean approach to criticism was far more systematic and disciplined than Lowell's critical method.

In May 1866, the Church brothers had offered Stedman the editorship of the *Galaxy* and urged him to "run their concern generally," as he reported to Taylor. It should have been possible for him to edit the magazine and have time for his own writing, as

Howells would be able to do as editor with the *Atlantic*. However, for "various reasons"—left unspecified—he declined. Doubtless Colonel Church would not have offered his friend a responsible position if he could not pay a living wage. Stedman may well have been drawn to Wall Street instead by the memory of the large sums he had obtained so easily but a few years earlier. Having retained his seat on the Government Bond Board, it was relatively easy for him to resume business. Thus, he passed up a potentially significant editorial assignment.

But he found a far more treacherous stock market, one that demanded his most strenuous efforts simply to survive. Late in 1867 he had to borrow from his wealthy uncle William Dodge to stay in business. As he continued to lose money, he sold his paintings, moved to cheaper accommodations in New Jersey, and even, for a time, sent his children to live with Laura's family in Connecticut. Ironically, he turned to literary work to help make ends meet. Late in 1868 he agreed, on a private basis, to help George P. Putnam edit the recently revived *Putnam's*. He described the unique relationship to Taylor, who contributed a regular column on European literature:

Now, as he cannot afford to regularly employ me as editor—as [James T.] Fields employs Howells—to receive all Mss., order fresh matter, read proofs, & do the whole work at a fair salary;—in short, as I cannot have all the responsibility, & as he has got himself into a bad snarl by having accepted *files* of poor matter, which must be got rid of etc,—I am unwilling to accept any public editorship or any responsibility, except for my specialty of book reviews. [43]

Stedman did conduct the "literature" section, writing four or five pages of book reviews each month, but clearly he was not the responsible editor of the magazine, as has been claimed by Frank Luther Mott. [44]

Stedman ended the *Putnam's* connection in May 1869, after the Regular Stock Exchange offered to admit members of the Bond Board to the Exchange at the bargain price of $1,000. Since Exchange seats had been selling for $10,000, Stedman suddenly found himself about $9,000 richer and this became the "turning point" in his life "as regards the question of subsistence" (I, 433). The seat served at once as a life insurance policy and a means of earning a living. Although Stedman was to speak at various times of his desire to obtain a regular salaried position, the many offers he did receive—like the editorship of the *Galaxy* or, much later, endowed chairs at Columbia and at Yale—invariably came too early or too late. Following a brief period of prosperity after joining the Regular Exchange, Stedman's "hateful" business once again became only marginally profitable. He was, after all, but a small operator in a chaotic, virtually unregulated securities market dominated by the likes of Jim Fisk and Jay Gould. In October 1870, a forgery of some $20,000 nearly destroyed his firm and simply "unhinged" him (I, 445). Business demanded his constant attention, but he could barely make a living. And there were other disappointments. In August 1869, Laura nearly died in giving birth to a "beautiful" daughter, but the girl did not survive. A few months later the couple were drugged with chloroform during a robbery of their home. So despondent did he become that he confessed to Taylor that he was "falling into an apathy with regard to anything beautiful or strong, and take no pleasure in *enjoyment* of intellectual spectacle; i.e. I am too *distrait* to seek enjoyment, even of the kind most desirable to me" (I, 446). Life was but a succession of "*prolonged* reverses . . . literary, pecuniary, and what-not" (I, 441). Composition became virtually impossible.

His depression was deepened by his inability to find a way to respond adequately to what he called the "wretched, immediate *fashion* of this demoralized American period," as he characterized the literary situation in an 1873 letter to Taylor in Germany (I, 477). The postwar literary market was burgeoning, but the new mass culture also seemed to bring a disturbing decline of standards, especially among younger readers. This generation "have tired of the past, and don't see clearly how to shape a future; and so content themselves with . . . applauding slang and nonsense, spiced with smut and profanity." Such "cultured" writers as John Hay and Bret Harte are "almost equally responsible with 'Josh Billings' and the 'Danbury News Man' " (I, 477). He formulated a sensible strategy for dealing with this new world, "adopt their system, and *elevate* it," but in practice, his ambivalence and irritation about the entire subject prevented him from either recognizing the genuine value of some of the new work, such as Hay's *Pike County Ballads,* or actually working in this genre himself (I, 477–78). In 1871, in speaking of the great popularity of Harte's "Heathen Chinee," he observed, "The worst of it is that every scribbler undertakes the same thing—to say nothing of some true men—and none of us hereafter will dare to paint *genre* pictures, for fear of counting in that crowd. I have had a dialect poem in my desk for years, called 'Old Hankes,' which now I shall certainly not print, even if I finish it" (I, 449).

Stedman might have capitalized on this market if he had decided to exploit his talent for comic verse. On a few occasions he wavered, as when he composed "The House that Vander Bilt" for $100.00 at the urging of Henry Bowen, editor of the *Independent*. [45] But he felt guilty about this "fall," and, as he recorded in his diary, he rejected Bowen's offer that he write "twelve more such 'poems' for the next year. . . . As if I were a grist-mill, or J. G. Saxe!" (I, 439).

Still, it bothered him to see the extravagant rewards granted work that he considered subliterary. In fact, he could not help but feel squeezed between the newer popularizers, on the one hand, and the older, established New England traditionalists on the other. While he published traditional poetry for good prices in the best magazines, he shared with Taylor a sense that their work did not speak to a broad audience, in the manner of Whittier, or Longfellow, or Emerson, or even Holmes. Paradoxically, he felt that he deserved greater popularity—"a little of the *popularis aura* is my right, and would do me good"—and that he was far from having done his best work (I, 478).

Part of the difficulty may be traced to the nature of the magazine poem as Stedman conceived it. He believed in the primacy of the long poem on some noble subject. (Hence, the lifelong search for—and lament at never finding—a suitable theme). On May 1, 1868, in writing privately to the *Nation* in response to some rather disparaging remarks on one of his *Scribner's* poems, made in the course of a typically caustic review of recent American literary magazines, he described the plight of the "conscientious American artist":

He may be at work, patiently and lovingly, on some "sustained" and larger effort, and at the same time often be willing or compelled to sell those little sketches which, however complete in themselves, are not his important work, but merely the reflections of varying phases, etc. Now if, in selling these little money-getters, he is not tempted into sensationalism,—if he never betrays his sacred calling,—if he does no *slovenly* work, but finishes sweetly and carefully even his trifles,—he is not to be condemned, nor estimated solely by these trifles. The question should be—Has the writer of this lyric done what he purposed to do? Has he, on the whole, been true to himself, and also met the want of the publisher and public? (I, 423)

Unfortunately, as an objective poet, Stedman resisted the idea that the poems reflecting the artist's "varying phases" may compose his most important work. He was unwilling, perhaps afraid, to undertake, as Whitman had done, the difficult task of exploring the self. In *Victorian Poets* he insists that subjective poetry is the proper sphere of female artists. And he did not absorb the lesson of his master, Tennyson, who "put into short pieces . . . what most of his forerunners would have spun into long poems."[46] Consequently it was all too easy to think of the "magazine poem" as a lesser genre.

He grew tired of producing "magazine poems," observing to Taylor in November 1872 that he "could write a lyric per week, but do not see the use of writing any more lyrics. I wish to do some larger work, but am oppressed with the old trouble, *lack of theme*" (I,464). He confessed to William Winter early in 1873 that he shared with him "a sense of failure in literature" (I,466). Similarly, in October 1874 he wrote Howells, "You *know* I can write correct, finished, aesthetic sonnets and quatrains,—can do it every day, but am tired of such work" (I,524). Business troubles exacerbated the problem; early in 1871 he described himself as enduring "a chronic state of alarm (business matters scare me—I can never get used to them)" (I,449).

But he refused to give up entirely, and told Taylor in October 1872 of a glimmer of hope "that the track of my mind-revolution will yet cross that of the world's real, practical literary work." He would be willing to "change my whole mode of life," if he "could only . . . hit upon the course of some congenial and noble enterprise" (I,464). He recognized, as he wrote William Winter in January 1873, that he possessed a "kind of dogged, critical faculty within me," and sought to analyze the social and literary factors that were responsible for the "sense of failure in literature" which he shared with him (I,466). In "Tennyson and Theocritus," he once again examined the modern stylistic problem from the perspective of the overrefined, overcultured Alexandrian Age. He thought of the essay, which appeared in the *Atlantic* for November 1871, as a kind of trial run before beginning a series on the leading Victorian poets. Encouraged by the response, he began work on the project in the summer of 1872, while on vacation in Plymouth, Massachusetts. His travel letters, "Old Colony Papers," for the *Tribune*, now edited by one of his closest friends, Whitelaw Reid, helped cover his expenses. His success in business the next fall enabled him to save some money. At the beginning of 1873 he suddenly and courageously decided to leave business and devote the year to literature—whatever the financial consequences. Through literary criticism he would attempt to "cross [the track] of the world's real, practical literature work" (I,464).

CHAPTER 2

The New Criticism

I The Critical Moment

UNDER the title "Victorian Poets" *Scribner's Monthly* for January 1873 carried a preliminary version of the first chapter of the book that would become *Victorian Poets*. Nine essays followed in *Scribner's* over the next three years. Stedman devoted separate chapters to Landor, both Brownings, Tennyson, and Swinburne; Hood, Arnold, and Procter were considered together, as were Buchanan, Rossetti, and Morris. The series concluded with the two part "Minor Victorian Poets." Stedman and Howells had had a tentative agreement to publish the series in the *Atlantic*, which had carried "Tennyson and Theocritus," also included in the volume. But Howells rejected the Landor essay because it was written "solely for literary men, and for mighty literary men at that" and "Victorian Poets" because he could not "see its necessity in the magazine, though it would properly introduce the other essays in a book."[1] With that, Stedman transferred the series to the popular New York monthly. *Victorian Poets*, published late in 1875 by James R. Osgood in Boston and by Chatto and Windus in London, is the first comprehensive history of Victorian poetry. As the first extended demonstration of Tainean critical principles by an American, it marked the beginning of a new approach to criticism in America.

Since the book incorporates Taine's central insight that in Stedman's words, "an author is governed by his period,"[2] it is particularly appropriate, before discussing it, to place Stedman's critical philosophy within the context of the postwar period. I have already mentioned the growing recognition of criticism itself. Such great editors as E. L. Godkin of the *Nation*, J. G. Holland of *Scribner's*, Howells of the *Atlantic*, and Lowell of the *North American* made ample space available both for practical criticism and more general discussions that turned on the question of "American

Criticism: Its Difficulties and Prospects," to use the title of Charles Astor Bristed's essay in the *North American* for January 1872. As the limitations of American criticism were identified, it was generally recognized that its prospects were dependent, among other things, upon the ability of American critics to absorb the lessons of such Europeans as Taine, Arnold, and Sainte-Beuve. As Stedman wrote in January 1873: "of late, and chiefly through translations from the French and German, the public mind has become somewhat aware of the advances made in the direction of true criticism, and acknowledges the philosophical character of a method signally illustrated, for example, by M. Taine."[3] To catch up with European "advances," American criticism would have to become more "philosophical," carefully define its premises, and then proceed objectively and consistently. In broader terms, as Howard Mumford Jones has observed, such "genteel critics" as Stedman, Howells, George Woodberry, Richard W. Gilder, Brander Matthews, James Huneker, and William Cary Brownell "took with admirable seriousness the injunctions of Goethe and Arnold that, if one wished to avoid provinciality, one must become a good European."[4]

The two European critics who exerted the greatest influence in America, Taine and Arnold, preeminently represented qualities of order, lucidity, and proportion. And these were precisely the qualities that many younger critics were attempting to express in their work and, in turn, to inculcate in American literature at large. For instance, in a review for *Putnam's* of Taine's *Ideal in Art*, Stedman contrasts Taine's disciplined critical method with Ruskin's lack of self-restraint. He praises the French critic for never leaving "his proper business, the logic and progress of the investigation. He thus exhibits a self-restraint which Ruskin, for example, fails of . . . . Taine has the faculty of rejecting details, except those positively required for illustration; and these, selected from the most prominent types, are generally absolute and convincing."[5] R. H. Stoddard at the end of an essay on Arnold, expressed the "wish" "that we had a writer like Mr. Arnold in this country (even if a poet were spoiled in making him), a scholarly and conscientious man of letters, who would devote himself to the examination of our authors, and to the destruction of their . . . thousand faults of temper and taste. We must have an American critic, if we are to have an American literature; for, when the age of creative energies is past . . . there can be no literature without criticism."[6] This call, published early in 1870, would be support enough for Stedman's decision to devote his literary energies to criticism instead of poetry. Stoddard's essay was the first in a "Victorian" series for *Appleton's* in which he also considered Swinburne, Procter, Ruskin, Browning, and Tennyson. The series may well have suggested to Stedman the possibility of doing an integrated study of current British poetry.

The particular quality of Stedman's concern for craftmanship in criticism is revealed in his argument, in *Poets of America*, that certain of the essays of Lowell "fall short in construction; they are not sustained upon the scales indicated at commencement. . . . His mind seizes upon a great theme, in mass and in detail, and he begins as if to cover it thoroughly. . . . But to complete an essay upon this plan a book must be written."[7] I am not implying that Stedman's own work invariably is a model of constructive power. But, as this comment suggests, he consciously sought to work within an ordered structure; the individual chapters of his major critical works are both complete essays within themselves and integrated parts of a coherent book. Although he did not begin with a master plan, his three critical volumes, *Victorian Poets, Poets of America,* and *The Nature and Elements of Poetry,* pursue a single subject, defining a comprehensive theory of poetry and evaluating the most important modern poetry written in English.

II *Science and Criticism*

The concern for defining clear and consistent critical principles was closely related to the growing postwar interest in science. One could not ignore the technological advances that were transforming everyday life. But public discussion also extended to the nature of scientific thinking and the changes the new science was bringing to education. "The truth is," Stedman wrote in *Victorian Poets,* "our school-girls and spinsters wander down the lanes with Darwin, Huxley, and Spencer under their arms; or if they carry Tennyson, Longfellow, and Morris, read them in the light of spectrum analysis, or test them by the economics of Mill and Bain" (13). That Stedman could casually note that "criticism, like science," had recently found a more interested public suggests that the interest in science was taken for granted and that there was an implicit connection between the two. The country was trying to recover from a tragic civil war caused, many people felt, by extremes of unchecked passion, and the precise, objective thinking associated with the scientific method offered a corrective. *Appleton's* defined the question in 1869:

It has been found that there are two kinds of knowing; we may know a subject loosely and vaguely, or with clearness and precision. So important has this distinction now become, that it is necessary to mark it in language, and so the word science has come to be applied to one of those kinds of knowledge; it means to know *accurately*.[8]

The writer, most likely *Appleton's* editor, Edward Livingston Youmans, challenges workers in all fields of intellectual endeavour to proceed systematically, to search constantly for the basic laws of the discipline. Stedman explained in his preface that the purpose of *Victorian Poets* was not only to evaluate the work of a group of poets, but also to express "incidentally such ideas concerning the aim and constituents of Poetry as I have gathered during my acquaintance with the historic body of English verse. Often, moreover, a leading author affords an illustration of some special phase of the poetic art and life" (x). Stedman sought to write a criticism that would be at once practical in its evaluation of the work of both major and minor poets, and theoretical in its search for basic principles.

Further, science now challenged the critic to explore from a new perspective the basic principles of literary expression, particularly the problem of the relationship of the work of art to the social and historical environment. In the most comprehensive study of the subject, Harry Hayden Clark has written that "the philosophical and sociological implications of evolution," certainly the most important of the new scientific ideas, "gradually led people . . . to try to explain literary art and creativeness in terms of the physiological-psychological study of the individual considered as determined by both heredity and environment, by time, place, and race."[9] More than any other critic, Taine, in his large philosophical scope and in his treatment of literature as an expression of a changing, evolving human society, seemed to incorporate this new perspective. A translation of his *History of English Literature* was published in America late in 1871, prompting a wide-ranging discussion of the purposes of literary criticism. For Stedman, this discussion could not have come at a more opportune time.

In what is probably the best of the American reviews of Taine's book, T. R. Lounsberry, writing in the *Nation* for January 4, 1872, condemned the usual chronicle type of literary history as "full of information, but of information ill-arranged, ill expressed, utterly undigested. Masses of fact are heaped together without any logical sequence, without any thread of connection save that of time—an

important one, certainly, but by no means the most important." But
Taine's challenging work opened entirely different possibilities, by
placing literary history within the realm of philosophical inquiry and
the "history of ideas":

It is a scientific exposition of the changes that have taken place in the
intellectual development of a people, the causes which have led to them, the
results that have sprung from them. Its chief aim is to trace those principles of
thought and action which, ruling the lives of men, have found expression in
their literature. . . . Literature is bound up with the national life, and, in
order to know the characteristic of the one it is essential to study closely the
other. Race, climate, political institutions, manners, and customs, all
become of importance.[10]

It was not that Lounsberry, or, for that matter, very many American
critics, accepted Taine on every point. Lounsberry, for instance,
condemned his mechanical application of certain questionable
scientific ideas to literature and argued that the ideal literary history
should contain more of the essential literary "facts" than Taine had
supplied. And Stedman rejected much of Taine's pseudoscientific
baggage by ignoring it. But after Taine, literary history would have to
be written from a philosophical perspective—it would have to have
ideas—and it would have to relate literature to the broader
intellectual environment.

III   Victorian Poets

In the context of the realism-idealism debate, *Victorian Poets* had a
surprising impact. This popular volume went through twenty
editions between 1875 and 1891 and so helped make Taine's scientific
realism better known. And through its sympathetic treatment of
beauty in such poets of the "art-school" as Landor, Tennyson,
Swinburne, and Rossetti, the book attacked the moralism of the New
England critical tradition. Since *Scribner's Monthly* was edited by
one of the leading exponents of this tradition, Dr. Josiah G. Holland,
Stedman's defense of beauty was all the more effective.

A close reading of *Victorian Poets* within the context of contemporary criticism demonstrates the continuing strength of the influence of
British poets in America at this time and provides new insight into
their competing reputations, particularly those of Browning and
Tennyson. With the minor exception of Procter and the major
exceptions of Arnold and, in part, of Browning, Stedman's insights

largely anticipate the modern consensus. As Jerome Buckley has recognized, *Victorian Poets* is a book with continuing relevance to the methodological problems of students of the period: Stedman was "less reluctant than some later critics to reach general conclusions. . . . His criticism, Arnoldian as it is in tone, relates Victorian poetry to the context of an analytic age and emphasizes a problem still too often neglected by the scholar: the problem of style, which in some form or other has faced all poets since the time of the Romantics."[11]

Stedman begins by explicitly accepting the core of Taine's theory, that the critic must account for the complex interrelationship of writer and environment, the "insensible moulding of an author's life, genius, manner of expression, by the conditions of race, circumstance, and period, in which he is seen to be involved" (1). Later in the chapter he affirms the more basic idea that the artist too must deal creatively with his own moment, insisting that "the most important art of any period is that which most nearly illustrates its manners, thoughts, and emotions in an imaginative language or form" (27).

Still, Stedman rejects the full deterministic implications of Taine's theory; the successful work of art is not simply a reflection of environment. For Stedman was centrally concerned with what he saw as a uniquely modern situation, the plight of the artist in an antagonistic environment. Here, the artist, while attempting to encompass the essential features of the period in his work, must at the same time struggle against the period or be overwhelmed by it. But only the poets of true genius are able to "overcome all restrictions, create their own styles, and even . . . determine the lyrical character of a period, or indicate that of one which is to succeed them." "Genius . . . is largely independent of place or time" (1–2). Stedman's inherited idealism, then, prevented him from falling into the deterministic trap of Taine's aesthetic system.

This argument led Stedman directly to his definition of the "twofold" nature of the critic's "province":

He must recognize and broadly observe the local, temporal and generic conditions under which poetry is composed, or fail to render adequate judgment upon the genius of the composer. Yet there always are cases in which poetry fairly rises above the idealism of its day. The philosophical critic, then, in estimating the importance of an epoch, also must pay full consideration to the messages that it has received from poets of the higher rank, and must take into account the sovereign nature of a gift so independent and spontaneous that from ancient times men have united in looking upon it as a form of inspiration.(4)

Certainly Stedman did not offer a detailed analysis of all the intellectual problems raised by Taine, and his theory is not a complex application of a set of ideas to literary study. But in formulating the problem in this way, he established a clear theoretical framework that enabled him to get on with the important critical job at hand.

It also enabled him to respond to what Robert Falk has called the "essential problem of intellectual America between 1871 and 1891," the "conflict of science and materialism with the inherited ideals of the Enlightenment and the traditional American faith in the individual. The ideological effort in those two decades strove to come to terms with the menace of a mechanistic world-view without wholly yielding up the inherited idealism of the earlier nineteenth century."[12] This problem was to concern Stedman throughout his career. Clearly Stedman did not, as has been charged, react to these problems in an ostrichlike manner, simply hoping that they would go away: the second section of this chapter studies the effects upon the poetic imagination of "the scientific movement which has engrossed men's thoughts, and so radically affected their spiritual and material lives, [that it] assumes an importance equal to that of all other forces combined" (7).

Although the conflict between the new science and traditional religion was then a subject of widespread debate and analysis, Stedman felt that the impact of science "upon poetry, through antagonism to the traditional basis of poetic diction, imagery, and thought," had received little, if any, recognition (7). Four years later, the distinguished Irish critic Edward Dowden, in "The Scientific Movement in Literature," in explaining why any investigation into the subject must be "guided by hints, signs, and presages," observed, "the time has not yet come when it may be possible to perceive in complete outline the significance of science for the imagination and the emotions of men."[13]

Even before beginning his analysis, however, Stedman professed his faith that the "antagonism" between science and the poetic imagination was not "inherent," that the conflict was "temporary." Like Wordsworth and Whitman, he expected that the two ultimately would be reconciled, leading to "new and fairer manifestations of the immortal Muse." In fact, the scientific movement had already been helpful in allowing man to rid himself of certain "ancient fables and follies of expression" (8). However, Stedman's confidence in an ultimate solution did not lead him to underestimate the seriousness of the immediate problem.

He argues that poetry had lost much of its traditional authority, and that individual poets had suffered a corresponding loss of confidence in the importance of their work. As a result of a radical epistemological shift, from "the poetic, or phenomenal mode" of perception to "the rational, or scientific mode," the poet can no longer be certain that the world as he views it directly is the "real world" (9,15). Now natural phenomena must be understood not as they seem to the unaided eye but in relation to complex, always changing scientific hypotheses discovered through complex instruments and recorded in special languages. The effect of the new theories of the universe, in which man no longer plays the central role, has been to "repress self-assertion, and to make one content with accepting quietly his little share of life and action" (12). What has been lost is not religious faith alone, but a unified world view. Yet, such a world picture has been an essential feature of the greatest creative periods: "Great productions usually have been adjusted to the formulas of some national or world-wide faith, and its common atmosphere pervades them" (18).

Further, modern society is essentially prosaic, lacking the mystery, strangeness, and imaginative speculation of certain earlier periods. It is an almost unreal period of "repose and luxury," the "noonday of common-sense, breeding, facts as they are" (23,24). Sadly, "even the poets, with their intensely sympathetic natures, have caught the spirit of the age, and pronounce the verdict against themselves. . . .Science, the modern Circe, beguiles them from their voyage to the Hesperides, and transforms them into her voiceless devotees" (13,14). Lacking a vital subject matter, then, modern poetry is content "to wreak its thoughts upon expression," and confines itself to the "skilful utilization of the laws of form and melody" (13).

Stedman's central concern as a critic is with the problem of style, and in the last section of the chapter he shows how the new "scientific iconoclasm" has influenced poetic diction, imagery, and thought. When written out of a unified world view, poetry could devote itself equally to truth and beauty. But as a result of its loss of authority, a tension between these two elements emerged at the outset of the Victorian period. Two competing traditions became evident: "the first was that of an art-school, taking its models from old English poetry and from the delicate classicism of Landor and Keats; the second was of a didactic, yet elevated nature, and had the imaginative strain of Wordsworth for its loftiest exemplar" (4). Since the Victorian poets often lacked strong and vibrant subject matter, and since they were less concerned with the "truth" of their statements than with "beauty" of expression, they concentrated on developing technique, creating a composite school. The work of this tradition should not be "underestimated." However, in the early work of Swinburne, "a phenomenal genius, the extreme product of the time," it has been carried "to that excess which foretokens exhaustion." Stedman predicts the eventual emergence of a "dramatic, spontaneous" poetry. But for now, the dominant conventions of Victorian poetry—conventions through which he had formed his own style and in which he continued to work—had been exhausted. It was time, then, to pause and consider the origins and development of Victorian poetry, and Stedman begins with an unlikely figure, Walter Savage Landor.

IV *Landor*

Under the usual laws of literary history, Landor should be treated with the Romantics. Stedman, who had begun to read him appreciatively as a student at Yale, may have been led to think of him as a contemporary by the fact that his mother had enjoyed a lively friendship with him in Florence, in the late 1850s and early1860s. But Stedman's essential purpose is to demonstrate a stylistic connection between Landor and contemporary poetry. Although chronologically a contemporary of the Romantics, Landor

stood among these, but not of them; greater or less, but different, and with the difference of a time then yet to follow. His style, thought, and versatility were Victorian rather than Georgian; they are now seen to belong to that school of which Tennyson is by eminence the representative. So far as his manner was anything save his own, it was that of recent years; let us say, instead, that the popular method constantly approached Landor's until the epoch of his death,—and he died but even now, when it is on the point of yielding to something, we know not what. . . . Passages are easily traceable where his art, at least, has been followed by poets who themselves have each a host of imitators. He may not have been the cause of certain phenomena; they may have sprung from the tendency of the age,—if so, he was the first to catch the tendency. (34–35)

Viewed historically, Landor could be "rescued" from his seemingly anomalous position and recognized as the progenitor of the art-school, "the first to honor his work with all the finish that a delicate ear and faultless touch could bestow upon it" (45).

Stedman's argument is not that, if better known, Landor would become a great popular favorite, or even that Landor's achievement was of the highest order. His work is "deficient in that broad human sympathy" that enabled, say, Shakespeare to win universal favor. "Landor belonged, in spite of himself, to the Parnassian aristocracy; was . . . a poet for poets" (37). But instead of pronouncing this a fatal weakness, as have most critics, Stedman proceeds to search for the stylistic qualities that such poets as Shelley, Southey, Wordsworth, Browning, Byron, and Swinburne have found so valuable for their own work. And we might add to this list, from the perspective of an additional one hundred years, Hopkins, Pound, Yeats, and Frost.

Landor's intense concern for style is evident in his first mature work, *Gebir*, a poem in which "art, treatment, imagination are everything; argument very little." Stedman correctly points out that "this strangely modern poem, which . . . has so much of Tennyson's finish, of Arnold's objectivity, and the romance of Morris and Keats," "had much to do with the inception and development of the Victorian School (40–41).[14] But Stedman credits the *Hellenics,* poems on classical themes written in the classical manner, with having exerted an even stronger influence, anticipating "a taste" which "has seized upon many a British poet." A committed classicist himself, Stedman treats Landor as an example of a writer whose use of the classics has enabled him to develop and strengthen his own style. In the *Hellenics,* "the Greek manner and feeling are veritably *translated*" (44). The same perfection of workmanship is to be found in the "numberless" "minor lyrics, epigrams, fragments" (46). In 1874, Stedman and Aldrich edited *Cameos,* their selection of the best of Landor's shorter works, calling attention to that portion of his work upon which his reputation chiefly rests today. It is, then, primarily as a stylist that Landor achieves his unique position (45).

Yet, citing Landor's own requirement that to earn the epithet "great" the poet must treat "a great subject worthily," Stedman argues that he did not attain the highest level (49). His natural abilities were dramatic, but the age did not provide him with the opportunity of writing dramas for stage presentation, and he suffered from "the one great want of many a master-mind . . . the lack of theme" (49). Once he discovered the appropriateness of the prose

dialogue in the *Imaginary Conversations* he was able to give full
expression to his dramatic sense, touching upon all subjects,
"everything to which human faculties have applied themselves" (50).
So highly does Stedman rank his masterpiece in this form, "Pericles
and Aspasia," that he would use it as an Arnoldian touchstone, "to test
the fabric of a person's temper by his appreciation of such a book"
(54). While Stedman does not confuse poetry and prose, he argues
that Landor's best "prose . . . is more imaginative than other men's
verses. Radically a poet, he ranks among the best essayists of his
time." In developing a new genre, the prose dialogue, to give
utterance to his dramatic sense, Landor serves as an example of an
artist able to overcome the inherent limitations of his time.

In the second and concluding division of the essay, Stedman
examines the complex pattern of Landor's life. Significantly, he does
not follow the usual Victorian practice of judging the value of an
artist's work in relation to the moral qualities of his life. Observing
that "there has been much confusion of Landor's personal history
with his writings, and an inclination to judge the latter by the
former," he separates them: "The moment he regarded men and
things *objectively*, he was the wisest of his kind; and some fine instinct
mostly kept him objective in his poetry, while his personality
expended itself in acts and conversation. If he seldom did 'a wise
thing,' he as seldom wrote 'a foolish one' " (54,58). Although
Stedman's portrait of Landor is drawn with affection and even
reverence, he does not hide his personal failings. But through the
discipline and impersonality of his art, Stedman argues, Landor was
able to attain an objectivity, a detached wisdom, quite at variance
with the lack of self-control which at times characterized his life.

In *Literary Criticism in America,* George E. DeMille writes, "the
chapter on Landor, whom Stedman, both by his classical sympathies
and by his admiration for pure finish of form, was well-fitted to
appreciate, is at once Stedman's masterpiece, and the best critique of
Landor that I have seen."[15] Technically, however, this essay is
top-heavy, the serious literary criticism coming at the outset, the
attendant biographical and other considerations following, almost as
an afterthought. In later essays, Stedman reversed the procedure.
And, as he later admitted, the essay, especially at the beginning, is
overwritten. But it is a remarkable, even a brilliant achievement,
which may, perhaps, best be appreciated if compared to Ezra
Pound's remarks on Landor. In emphasizing the unique value of

Landor's style, both critics identify virtually the same quality: Stedman describes the verse as "terse, yet fluent" (46), Pound as possessing a "hardness which is not of necessity rugged." "The *cantable* quality never wholly deserts the verses of his shorter poems." Pound credits Landor with creating a style "so far ahead of his British times that the country couldn't contain him." "He was driving piles into mud, and preparing foundations—which have been largely unused by his successors."[16] The lasting critical significance of Stedman's essay, which is an excellent introduction to a poet neglected by all but poets, comes from its demonstration of the stylistic relationship of Landor's "foundations" and Victorian poetry.

V *Tennyson*

More than any other Victorian poet, Tennyson built upon the foundation of the art school, and Stedman treats him as the representative poet of his era, exerting a stylistic influence which was "almost unprecedently dominant, fascinating, extended" (151). According to the standard interpretation, the decline of Tennyson's influence in America did not begin until the appearance of his plays, starting with *Queen Mary*, in the summer of 1875. Before that, his "reputation was at its height."[17] Yet, at the outset of "Alfred Tennyson," first published in *Scribner's* for May 1874, Stedman reports that a pronounced reaction is already well under way: "Even of [his] serene beauty we are wearied; a murmur arises; rebellion has broken out; the Laureate is irreverently criticised, suspected, no longer worshipped as a demi-god" (151). This decline revealed, as Henry James noted the next year, an uncertain situation: "The young persons of thirty read Browning, and Dante Rossetti, and Omar Kheyam [sic]—and are also sometimes heard to complain that poetry is dead and that there is nothing nowadays to read."[18] The challenge to the critic, Stedman recognizes, is to step outside the current of fashions and attempt "to forestall . . . [the] judgment of posterity" (152). He seeks to evaluate Tennyson's poetry "not by our appetite for it, but by its inherent quality" (153). This is a worthy critical goal, and one which, in many respects, Stedman achieved. But let us not underestimate the strength of his continuing commitment to the Tennysonian tradition. In the growing prominence of Browning, whom he then considered an inexcusably careless workman, Stedman felt that the anti-Tennyson reaction had gone too far. He had not lost faith in the great tradition embodied by Tennyson, in which poetry is both true and beautiful, and so his comprehensive review of Tennyson's development is also a sympathetic defense of the tradition.

Since there had not yet been a study "adequately setting forth" Tennyson's "technical superiority," the major focus of both the comprehensive "Alfred Tennyson" and "Tennyson and Theocritus" is stylistic. "Tennyson and Theocritus" argues that the origins of the master's style are to be found in the idyll and little epic developed by Theocritus and his school. This influence is crucial; if Theocritus "had not sung as he sang, in Syracuse and Alexandria, two thousand years ago, it is doubtful whether modern English fancy would have been under the spell of that minstrelsy by which it was of late so justly and delightfully enthralled" (204).

In defining the Syracusan connection, Stedman expands the broad comparison between the culture of the Alexandrian and Victorian periods that he had drawn in "English Poetry of the Period," published in the *North American* in 1866. His characterization of the Alexandrian cultural situation is meant to apply directly to the modern:

There was a mob of gentlemen who wrote with ease. Tact and scholarship so abounded, that it was difficult to draw the line between talent and genius. We see a period of scholia and revised and annotated editions of the elder writers; wherein was done for Homer, Plato, the Hebrew Scriptures, what is now doing for Dante, Shakespeare, and Goethe. Philology came into being, and criticism began to clog the fancy. Schoell says that "the poets were deeply read, but wanting in imagination, and often also in judgment." It was impossible for most to rise above the influence of the time. Science, however, made great strides. In material growth it was indeed a "wondrous age,". . .[all manner of cultural and commercial endeavors] finding support in the luxurious, speculative, bustling, news-devouring hurly-burly of that strangely modern Alexandrian time. (205–206)

Poet, critic, translator, philogist, man of commerce, politics, and the press, Stedman could not help but see himself as a "man of talent" in the developing American analogue to ancient Syracuse—New York City. The important point here, however, is that as poetry had come to a virtual dead end in the Alexandrian period, so, at the end of the Romantic period, when Tennyson began, "literature drifted into an indecisive, characterless period" (206).

Theocritus, nurtured in rural Sicily, was able to find a style by going back to "nature, which he knew and reverenced well." Bringing his art into contact with native, primitive sources, the "rude island ditties and mimes" which he discovered, he created a new poetic form, the idyll, "little pictures of real life upon the hillside and in the town, among the high and low,—portraying characters with a few distinct touches in lyric, epic, or dramatic form, and often by a combination of the whole" (207). Similarly, Tennyson, in reacting against the decay of poetic values, "willingly yielded himself" to the influence of Theocritus and his co-workers, Bion and Moschus: "It has never left him, but is present in his latest and most sustained productions. But there is a difference between his maturer work— which is the adjustment of the idyllic method to native, modern conceptions, with a delightful presentation of English landscape and atmosphere, and the manners and dialects of English life—and the experimental, early poems, which were written upon antique themes" (210). The brilliant Canadian critic Marshall McLuhan has made essentially the same point in the course of his suggestive "Tennyson and the Romantic Epic". Basing his insights on J.W. Mackail's *Lectures on Greek Poetry* (1910), he observes, "it was a sure instinct which led Tennyson to devote himself to Theocritus and the idyll or little epic, for the conditions which had brought about the cultivation of the romantic or little epic in the Hellenic world were largely paralleled in England in the nineteenth century. . . .Theocritus. . .though hampered by erudition and excessive literary production, had been driven back to the roots of ritual and myth as the basis for art."[19]

Stedman shows that both in the larger matters of rhythmic structure and tone and the more "immediate coincidence of structure, language, and thought," Tennyson made pervasive use of Theocritus and his school (211). He does not attempt to be exhaustive, but only to cite enough specific parallels to establish his case. Most have been detected by later scholars. He does not charge Tennyson with plagiarism, but credits him with reviving the pastoral tradition. In returning directly to Greek sources, Tennyson was able to purify the decadent pastoral tradition of the "standard British poets," as it had come down "by a kind of filtration through the Latin medium" (232). This essay in comparative criticism, properly singled out by reviewers as one of the best in the book, shows that Stedman had a fine sense of the relationship of individual talent to the whole literature of Europe, if we may use Eliot's terms. McLuhan has a challenging footnote: " 'What we need,' wrote Ezra Pound in *The Spirit of Romance*, 'is a literary scholarship which will weigh Theocritus and Yeats in one balance.' "[20]

Stedman's major essay, "Alfred Tennyson" seeks to define the particular quality of his technical mastery. "In marked contrast to his fellows, and to every predecessor but Keats," Tennyson recognized that poetry is an "exquisite art" devoted to beauty (156). Here again it will be useful to compare Stedman's insights into Tennyson's metrical procedure with those of McLuhan, this time in his essay "Tennyson and Picturesque Poetry." Following Arthur Henry Hallam's treatment of Tennyson as a "Poet of Sensation," the title of his review of *Poems, Chiefly Lyrical* (1831) in *Gentleman's Magazine*, McLuhan speaks of Tennyson's "habitual definition of a moment of awareness in terms of objective landscape. . .of the landscape or episode which defines and concentrates an intense experience."[21] Similarly for Stedman, Tennyson is the acknowledged leader of "the art school: that is, of poets who largely produce their effect by harmonizing scenery and detail with the emotions or impassioned action of their verse" (159). In the volume of 1832 the mature Tennyson emerged:

The command of delicious metres; the rhythmic susurrus of stanzas whose every word is as needful and studied as the flower or scroll of ornamental architecture,—yet so much an interlaced portion of the whole, that the special device is forgotten in the general excellence; the effect of color, of that music which is a passion in itself, of the scenic pictures which are the counterparts of changeful emotions; all are here, and the poet's work is the epitome of every mode in art. Even if these lyrics and idyls had expressed nothing, they were of priceless value as guides to the renaissance of beauty. Thenceforward slovenly work was impossible, subject to instant rebuke by contrast. (158)

In reviewing Tennyson's development as a writer, Stedman, unlike most of his contemporaries, recognizes a steady "intellectual growth." He advanced the principle that "other gifts being equal," the poet who has the more vigorous mind will draw ahead of his fellows, and take the front position" (167). And in this regard he ranks him ahead of Arnold and Browning. He characterizes Tennyson's intellectual quality, especially as exhibited in *In Memoriam*, his most characteristic work, as of the type which questions and probes, directly confronting the fundamental problems of the day. The intellectual content does not conflict with the sensory. He is not an abstract system builder, but "follows the example of his generation, and the more faithfully gives voice to its spiritual questionings" (170). *In Memoriam* is "distinctively a poem of this century . . . displaying the author's genius in a subjective form" (168). While Stedman does not have space to develop this idea in detail, his insight here does "forestall [the] judgment of posterity." As Clyde de L. Ryals has observed: "Placed in proper historical perspective, Tennyson emerges as a superior intelligence, as a maker of symbols who is essentially modern."[22]

While enthusiastic, Stedman's "Tennyson" is not uncritical. With the exception of "Guinevere," the later *Idylls* do not measure up to the standard of the first four. The "public poems" of Tennyson's laureateship are simply not to be included with his serious work. The major limitations of Tennyson's poetry, such as the uniformity of style and failure to create truly dramatic portraits, are those of the idyllic method itself. Here Stedman makes a perceptive prediction: "It is not improbable that Tennyson may force himself to compose some notably dramatic work; but only through skill and strength of purpose" (191). *Queen Mary*, of course, appeared the next year.

Perhaps the most serious weakness of this essay is a response to certain individual poems that is overly sentimental, as when he writes that " 'Dora' is like a Hebrew pastoral, the paragon of its kind, with not a quotable detail, a line too much or too little, but faultless as a whole. Who can read it without tears?" (162). But for the most part, both in its judgments of specific works and its analyses of larger trends, the essay is remarkably sound. It is constructed with a disciplined order and compression that enables Stedman to deal with the entire range of Tennyson's poetry while placing the work within the context of his complex period.

VI *Browning*

While he called for a new, more dramatic poetry, Stedman's commitment to the stylistic standards of the art school did limit his ability to respond to the new. Such, at least initially, was the case with Browning, Tennyson's great Victorian rival, and the poet whom Stedman himself credits with being the "long-neglected progenitor" of a new dramatic school that had arisen in reaction to the "tranquillity of picturesque repose" characteristic of the idyllic school (320). But Browning's "aggressive" style, he argues, presents too great a "contrast to the refined art of our day." Instead of subordinating his material to the demands of a traditional, melodious poetic style, Browning reverses the procedure, "compelling beauty itself to suffer a change and conform to all exigencies" (303). Because of the primary importance of style in Stedman's aesthetic, he concludes that Browning's art is seriously flawed: "by his contempt of beauty, or inability to surely express it, [he] fails of that union of art and spiritual power which always characterizes a poet entirely great" (341).

It must be remembered that Stedman was writing at a time when Browning, after the great triumph of *The Ring and the Book* (1869), had published, in rapid succession, four volumes that show a distinct falling off in artistic power. And there is a good deal of merit in certain of Stedman's basic reservations. As George Saintsbury has written, " 'Less matter with more art' was the demand which might have been made of Mr. Browning from first to last, and with increasing instance as he became more popular."[23] Further, Stedman is consciously reacting against a growing tendency to revere Browning as a great sage or lawgiver, a tendency that was confirmed in the anguished response of certain reviewers of *Victorian Poets*. Horace Scudder, for instance, writing in the *Atlantic*, criticized Stedman for not realizing that Browning's poetry, "more than that of any other Victorian poet, [is] the embodiment not of the questions which have agitated the minds of Englishmen but of the solution of the questions."[24] It was well, then, at a time when reverence for Browning as prophet and sage was already manifest, to focus on the complex question of his stylistic procedures and technique. Stedman writes on the subject with insight, although he does not develop his observations to their logical conclusions.

The tone of the essay is all the more harsh because Stedman recognizes that Browning, while perfectly capable of using a traditional, melodious style with great success—"he can be very artistic with no loss of original power"—also insists on employing a difficult, unconventional style:

Unlike Tennyson, he does not comprehend the *limits* of a theme; nor has he an idea of the *relative importance* either of themes or details; his mind is so alert that its minutest turn of thought must be uttered; he dwells with equal precision upon the meanest and grandest objects, and laboriously jots down every point that occurs to him,—parenthesis within parenthesis,—until we have a tangle as intricate as the line drawn by an anemometer upon the recording sheet. The poem is all zigzag, criss-cross, at odds and ends,—and, though we come out right at last, strength and patience are exhausted in mastering it. Apply the rule that nothing should be told in verse which can be told in prose, and half his measures would be condemned; since their chief metrical purpose is, through the stress of rhythm, to fix our attention, by a certain unpleasant fascination, upon a process of reasoning from which it otherwise would break away. (304)

The identification of the two styles anticipates two of the best recent critical articles on the subject.[25] Unfortunately, it did not occur to him to consider the possible functional uses of such a style, particularly its value in exploring the subtle processes of the human mind. Paradoxically, Stedman, while praising Browning for discovering a new and important subject matter for poetry in his explorations of the psychological complexities of his characters, was unwilling to accept the implications for style of this subject matter. The modern reader, however, is quite willing to view sympathetically the use of prosodic and other devices that may have the effect of "forcing" him to comprehend characters and ideas which might otherwise be found "repulsive." In this instance, Stedman serves as an excellent example of the critic who, while capable of understanding a new stylistic or artistic procedure, rejects it because it does not conform to a preconceived standard.

Paradoxically, Stedman considered his Browning essay the "*deepest* of the series" and was surprised to find that "all the Browning men in England and the United States are furious because I venture to criticise their idol—and don't see that I have praised him also."[26] Much of the praise, and Stedman's most perceptive writing in the essay, comes in his definition of Browning's "special mission,"

exploring those secret regions which generate the forces whose outward phenomena it is for the playwrights to illustrate. He has opened a new field for the display of emotional power,—founding. . .a sub-dramatic school of poetry, whose office is to follow the workings of the mind, to discover the impalpable elements of which human motives and passions are composed . . . . modern genius chooses to seek for the under-currents of the soul rather than to depict acts and situations. (297)

Stedman, of course, could not have foreseen that Browning's "sub-dramatic school" of the dramatic monologue would assume, in the work of Pound, Eliot, Robinson, and others, a dominant position in the modern poetic tradition. But his understanding of the new genre is nonetheless sound. In fact, Pound used much the same language, in a 1908 letter to William Carlos Williams, to describe his own poetic goals:

To me the short so-called dramatic lyric—at any rate the sort of thing I do—is the poetic part of a drama the rest of which (to me the prose part) is left to the reader's imagination or implied or set in a short note. I catch the character I happen to be interested in at the moment he interests me, usually a moment of song, self-analysis, or sudden understanding or revelation. And the rest of the play would bore me and presumably the reader.[27]

In defining this new poetry, Stedman does make certain of the fundamental distinctions necessary to an understanding of Browning's innovations. He recognizes that, in the traditional sense, Browning is not a dramatic poet, one whose primary concern is the objective portrayal of action, but an essentially lyrical and subjective artist whose "personality is manifest in the speech and movement of almost every character of each piece" (296). And his treatment of such volumes as *Men and Women* (1855) and *Dramatis Personae* (1864), where Browning uses the dramatic lyric with most success, is sympathetic.

Yet the essay as a whole, largely as a result of Stedman's irritation with the "difficult" style, is highly uneven. It is interesting to note that virtually all of the critical writing of substance on Browning has been favorable. As one Browning scholar has observed, "those who think poorly of Browning have not attacked him but ignored him."[28] Perhaps even the "favorable" critics wisely followed the example of Henry James, who wrote Stedman: "I quite sympathize with you in your wonder that Browning should have never felt the intellectual comfort of 'a few grave, rigid laws.' But Browning's badness I have never professed to understand. I limit myself to vastly enjoying his goodness."[29] In his ambitious essay, Stedman attempted the difficult task of appreciating the "goodness" and exposing the "badness," and we have a flawed essay.

VII   *Swinburne*

In writing on Swinburne, Stedman is able to take up the more comfortable role of defender and appreciator, arguing that although a poet of unrivaled technical skills and the foremost of the younger school of British poets, Swinburne had been maligned because of the alleged immorality of certain poems in the "formative" *Poems and Ballads* (1866). So sharp was the contrast in tone that the *North American* observed, "we do not imagine that Mr. Stedman really intends to rank Mr. Swinburne's achievements so high, or Mr. Browning's so low, as he appears to do." This reviewer praises Browning as "the strongest, truest poet of the Victorians," and condemns Swinburne: "If Swinburne has sung sweetly of beautiful things, he has also raved foully of horrible things."[30] His supposition on Stedman's final estimate of Browning was right. In the 1887 "Supplement" to *Victorian Poets* and in *Nature and Elements* he attempts to correct earlier errors of tone and emphasis, treating Browning as the leading poet of the second part of the prolonged Victorian period, as Tennyson had been of the first. But the enthusiastic defense of Swinburne was no mistake. Stedman became, in the words of Clyde Kenneth Hyder, "the most effective American champion of Swinburne's poetry."[31]

During an interview conducted after Stedman's death, Howells recalled that in the immediate postwar period, Stedman and Stoddard had been "very much taken with" Swinburne. "He appealed to Stedman on the scholarly side, because he was a great Grecian."[32] Accordingly, it is likely that it was Lowell, not Stedman, who, in "editing" "English Poetry of the Period," had written that both *Atalanta* and *Chastelard* had been "sent forth in an experimental or impulsive mood" and that Swinburne had yet to "acquire an artistic purpose." But at least Lowell allowed Stedman to remark that so great was Swinburne's genius, "much of the immediate future of English poetry rests upon what he may yet elect to do."[33]

In November 1866, in the course of a chatty letter, Stedman, anxious to learn Lowell's opinions of *Poems and Ballads*, mentioned Grant White's recent defense of the book in the *Galaxy*. Replying the next day, Lowell exploded: "I have not yet seen Swinburne's new volume—but a poem or two from it which I have seen shocked me, and I am not squeamish. . . . I am too old to have a painted *hetaira* palmed off on me for a Muse, and I hold unchastity of mind to be worse than that of body."[34]

With a few exceptions, including Stoddard's fine general essay on Swinburne in *Appleton's* for April 2, 1870, the leading American critical journals shared Lowell's moralistic condemnation.

Despite his great respect for Lowell, Stedman refused to go along. In his Landor essay (May 1873), he had praised the "unselfish reverence" of the young Swinburne in visiting the dying Landor in Italy, and then used Swinburne's "In Memory of Walter Savage Landor" as an epigraph for *Cameos*. The two became friends, beginning a wide-ranging correspondence. Such was the warmth of their friendship that in 1875 Swinburne, despite his firm practice of not discussing his past life, honored a request from Stedman by writing a remarkably full and probing autobiographical letter, one of his most important personal revelations.[35] In a 1909 letter to Laura Stedman, Theodore Watts-Dutton called Swinburne's letters to Stedman, "by far the most interesting that Algernon ever wrote."[36]

From the outset of the Swinburne essay itself, Stedman takes the offensive, challenging especially those writers who have ignored this poet on moral grounds: "reflecting upon his genius and the chances of his future, it is difficult for any one to write with cold restraint who has an eye to see, an ear to hear, and the practice which forces an artist to wonder at the lustre, the melody, the unstinted fire and movement, of his imperious song" (379–80). In analyzing his remarkable "command over the unsuspected resources of a language," Stedman singles out his "unprecedented" powers of melody and rhythm: "It is safe to declare that at last a time has come when the force of expression can no further go" (382). Here Stedman develops the thesis, begun in the introductory chapter, that in this very mastery, Swinburne has carried expression to "fatiguing excess," in the early works by "cloying us with excessive richness of epithets and sound: in later works, by too elaborate expression and redundancy of treatment" (382). A new style is needed. But if forced to decide between the two major stylistic traditions, the art school, with its emphasis on beauty of expression, as represented by Swinburne, or the dramatic school of Browning, with its emphasis on content at the expense of expression, Stedman chooses the former: "while Browning's amplification is wont to be harsh and obscure, Swinburne, even if obscure, or when the thought is one that he has repeated again and again, always gives us unapproachable melody and grace" (382).

Stedman firmly resisted the directive of his editor, Dr. Holland, in a letter dated December 27, 1874, that he balance his praise with a "condemnation of the man's nastiness."[37] On the contrary, in response to the "overloud" outcry of the moralists, he points out that *Poems and Ballads,* the only volume to be so questioned, had been written before the respected *Atalanta,* and should be seen as a "formative" work. Despite its many flaws of style, the collection exhibits the "spirit . . . of unbounded freedom, of resistance to an established ideal," which Swinburne shared with Shelley, whose poetry had meant so much to him (391, 392).

In discussing *Atalanta,* Stedman corrects Lowell's modifications of his earlier essay, arguing that here Swinburne brought the classical form alive and that the experience of submitting himself to its rigorous demands had been beneficial to his art. Among Swinburne's poetic works, he singles out for special praise the choruses of *Atalanta*, the elegies, most especially "Ave Atque Vale," and some of the less doctrinaire poems of *Songs before Sunrise,* such as "Hertha," which has "so much lyric force and music united with condensed and clarified thought" (401). However, he points out, correctly, that much of this volume "is tumultuous and ineffective. The prolonged earnestness fags the reader" (400). In keeping with his earlier assertion that Swinburne would take a leading role in the inevitable dramatic revival, he pays close attention to the two dramas on Mary Stuart, *Chastelard* (1865) and *Bothwell* (1874), poems that today are largely unread if not actually unreadable. With the exception of an overenthusiastic response to these poems, Stedman's basic treatment of Swinburne's work is sound. Stedman's courageous championship of Swinburne struck a strong blow against the critical moralism expounded by Dr. Holland. Perhaps the best way to appreciate his contribution is to quote in full the letter of December 27, 1874 in which Holland attempted to convince Stedman to modify the essay:

My dear Stedman:—

I have been reading your paper on Swinburne. It is much the most enthusiastic of the papers you have written, and has the push in it of a man who is conscious that he differs a bit from his neighbors. The effect of the paper will be to set every young man and woman reading Swinburne, and a great mass of hot, young mind[s] will be certain to come in contact with all his smut—a material which I hold to be outlawed of art. I cannot express to you the detestation in which I hold the indecencies of erotic verse. Byron was burned into my young brain as with a hot iron, and I have cursed Don Juan ever since. I would not willingly be instrumental [in] leading them through my own experience. Certainly I would not without placing in their hands at the same time a strong corrective.

I shall publish your article just as it is, if you do not think with me that somewhere in it you should be more emphatic in your condemnation of the man's nastiness, for you must remember that the style of this article marks it as a defense and a defiance. It will make a great deal of talk, and the public judgment will be, as I think it ought to be, that your admiration of the man's wonderful power and skill has blinded your mind to his immoralities and his immoral influence. Perhaps I am squeamish, but I cannot help it. If I were publishing a literary periodical, that only found a literary audience, I would not say a word. We should all understand you, but I publish for the crowd, and they take you for their leader and hold you responsible for all nuances, and moral damage.

The article pleased Swinburne, who told Stedman it was "the most powerful as well as the most gratifying to me personally I ever read on the subject."[39]

VIII The "Fleshly School" in America

The chapter on Swinburne (XI) is the second of a two part essay on "The Latter-Day Singers." In the first part, after a summary review of the problems faced by younger poets in a situation "so oppressive that there is reason to believe it must be near an end," Stedman considers in some detail the work of three, Robert Buchanan, D. G. Rossetti, and William Morris (343). Buchanan is remembered today not for his verse but for his spiteful attack on Rossetti and the Pre-Raphaelites in his pamphlet, *The Fleshly School of Poetry and Other Phenomena of the Day* (1872). Of this grouping William Fredeman has observed, "one can only speculate on the reaction of the Pre-Raphaelites on finding themselves allied with the arch-enemy, Buchanan."[40] Stedman reported to Hall Caine "that Rossetti was annoyed" with being included with Buchanan, but he defended it as "a mere *exigency* of my book."[41] His purpose is not to compare, but to contrast the various methods employed by these poets in their struggle "to break through and out of the restrictions that surround them" (343). In fact, as part of the larger argument of the essay, he sought to draw the "sharpest possible contrast" between Buchanan's oppressive didacticism and the aesthetic integrity of Rossetti, Morris, and Swinburne.

It must be pointed out that in America Buchanan was once considered a potentially promising poet.[42] In 1865, Stoddard had listed him and Swinburne as "the two most promising, as they are certainly the most prominent, of the later Poets of England."[43] Stedman argues that he has not fulfilled this promise: because of his propagandistic zeal, "his impulse to handle every theme that occurs to him, and to essay all varieties of style, much of his poetry, even after the winnowing to which it has been subjected, is not free from sterile and prosaic chaff" (355). In thus disposing of the didactic Buchanan, Stedman can turn to the more sympathetic Pre-Raphaelites.

Buchanan's first attack on Rossetti had come in "The Fleshly School of Poetry," an extended review of *Poems* (1870).[44] The previous year, the leading English periodicals and reviewers had, of course, been enthusiastic—even wildly so. Rossetti himself had orchestrated this response. But in America the situation was decidedly different. The leading journals, the *Nation* (July 14), *North American* (October), *Harper's Monthly* (August), *Atlantic* (July), and the *Galaxy* (August) had focused, with varying degrees of emphasis, upon the sensual element as a defect in Rossetti's work. Accordingly, it was to America, and specifically to Boston, that Buchanan looked for support. In concluding, he asserted that his "judgment on Mr. Rossetti . . . is substantially that of the *North American Reviewer* [sic], who believes that we have in him another poetical man . . . so affected, sentimental, and painfully self-conscious, that the best to be done in his case is to hope that this book of his, having unpacked his bosom of so much that is unhealthy, may have done him more good than it has given others pleasure!"[45] While there were a few appreciative American reviews—in the failing *Putnam's*, by J. W. Stillman (July), in *Lippincott's* (September 1870), and in the New York *Times* (July 18, 1870)—the major periodicals reached a consensus that a poet so deeply enmeshed in the sensual could not create a spiritual, and hence a truly significant, art.

Directing his argument at precisely this point, Stedman contends that Rossetti and "his associates [are] humble lovers of the beautiful, first of all, and through its ministry . . . rise to the lustrous upper heaven of spiritual art" (366). And far from finding anything dangerous in Rossetti's verse, Stedman treats him as "an earnest and spiritual artist." In response to the argument that Rossetti's sensualism provides *prima facie* evidence that he could not be an artist of original or profound power, Stedman points to his position as the leading spirit of the Pre-Raphaelites and his "radical and more or less enduring" influence on such associates as Morris and Swinburne (357). But unlike his overly fluent contemporaries, his style is marked by "a finesse, a regard for detail, and a knowledge of color and sound, that distinguish this master of the Neo-Romantic school. His end is gained by simplicity and sure precision of touch" (361). Especially in view of the narrowly moralistic tone of earlier American criticism, Stedman's sensitive and perceptive response to this difficult poet represents one of the more important contributions of the volume.

By way of contrast, the third major Pre-Raphaelite poet, William Morris, was not considered an immoral writer in America. On the contrary, the publication of *The Earthly Paradise* (1868–1870) had brought him, in the words of *Harper's*, to "the front rank of modern poets."[46] The questions that were raised—and these were heard with increasing emphasis as the succeeding installments of the work were released—concerned the relative diffuseness of his verse. The

Atlantic, for instance, came to doubt whether "Mr. Morris is great in proportion to the bulk of his books."[47] With this basic view Stedman was in essential agreement: "The poetry of William Morris is thoroughly sweet and wholesome. . . . Yet it is but the choicest fashion of romantic narrative-verse. The poet's imagination is clear, but never lofty; he never will rouse the soul to elevated thoughts and deeds" (378). Dissatisfied with the "sweet, but unimpassioned, measures" of William Morris, Stedman, in concluding his essay, sounds again his call for a strongly dramatic poetry.

IX   *Matthew Arnold*

As a whole, "Thomas Hood—Matthew Arnold—Bryan Waller Procter" is the weakest essay of the book. Ostensibly, its purpose is not to judge these writers, but to contrast three very different yet representative poets as a means of illuminating the varying tendencies of the period. But whatever Stedman's stated intention, it is clear that in this grouping he was attempting to make a critical comment. As DeMille has put it, "one finds it hard to forgive his lumping together in one chapter, and treating as of equal value, Hood, Arnold, and Bryan Waller Procter."[48]

Today, Arnold's position as a major Victorian poet is secure, Hood is emerging as a "Victorian Forerunner," to use the title of John Chubbe's fine book, and Procter, quite properly, has been all but forgotten.[49] In the "Supplement" (1887) Stedman reevaluated these poets. He confesses in his new "Preface"

that the prominence given to Procter seems hardly in accord with the just perspective of a synthetic view. It grew out of the writer's distaste for two characteristics of latter day verse: on the one hand, the doubt and sadness of that which is the most intellectual; on the other, the artificial tone of that offered by many younger poets, in whom the one thing needful seemed to be the spontaneity so natural to "Barry Cornwall." [Procter's pen name.]
    While I thought the first of these characteristics too excessive in the poetry of Arnold. . .I paid full tribute to the majesty of his epic verse. But I was unjust in a scant appreciation of what is after all his most ideal trait, and his surest warrant as a poet. For this fault I now make reparation in the supplement. (vii–viii)

Stedman had attempted to use the example of Procter to demonstrate that the artist could escape the weariness and disquiet characteristic of Arnold's subjective poetry.

The original essay had sought to maintain that Arnold's "sadness and doubt [is] an unconscious confession of his own special restrictions,—restrictions other than those which, as he perceives, belong to England in her weary age, or those which, in a period of transition from the phenomenal to the scientific, are common to the whole literary world" (95). It is as if the tone of these poems was too threatening for Stedman personally and in response he moved to banish all such subjective poetry. In this, his reaction may be compared to Arnold's own decision, as explained in his "Preface" to *Poems* (1853), not to include "Empedocles on Etna" because it would not "inspirit and rejoice the reader."[50] "When Arnold adopts these judgments," Walter Houghton has observed in *The Victorian Frame of Mind*, "we have to remember how strongly the burden of depression could reinforce the demand for moral optimism."[51] A similar point should be made about Stedman, and this helps explain the "Arnoldian" tone of his criticism.

In describing Arnold's goal as "spiritualizing what he deems an era of unparalleled materialism" and his plight as that "of a thoughtful man, who in vain longs to create some masterpiece of art, and whose yearning and self-esteem make him loath to acknowledge his limitations, even to himself," Stedman is also suggesting something of his own predicament (97). The "objective method," Stedman asserts, "is well suited to a man of large or subtle intellect and educated tastes, who is deficient in the minor sympathies. Through it he can allow his imagination full play, and give a pleasure to readers without affecting that feminine instinct which really is not a constitnent of his poetic mould" (93). We have the remarkable identification of the subjective and personal with the feminine: apparently Stedman was afraid that if he expressed the frustrations and resentments of his life, he would be overwhelmed, rendered helpless, vulnerable, emasculated. But in the supplementary chapter for *Victorian Poets*, and in *The Nature and Elements of Poetry*, Stedman reverses himself, recognizing that the artist cannot create according to some abstract theory that is not true to his inner being. Specifically, he finds that Arnold's best work is not the blank verse studies, where he effaces himself, but

the poetry wherein he. . .most entirely and unreservedly expressed himself. . .the tender, personal, subtly reflective lyrics that seem like tremulous passages from a psychical journal; most of all, perhaps, for those which so convey the spirit of youth,—the youth of his own doubting,

searching, freedom-sworn Oxonian group—a group among whom he and
Clough. . .were leaders in their search for unsophisticated nature and life, in
their regret for inaction, their yearning for new light, their belief that love
and hope are the most that we can get from this mortal existence. [52]

The section on Hood, the most balanced and perceptive of the
three, is an attempt to define Hood's position as a uniquely modern
poet. While Stedman recognizes the value of such early traditional
lyrics as "Fair Ines," "The Plea," and "Lycus the Centaur," he argues
that Hood's most important contribution, his most characteristic
work, was done within the last few years of his life in such works as
"The Lay of the Laborer," "The Lady's Dream," "The Bridge of
Sighs," and "Song of the Shirt." Hood brought into poetry a whole
new subject matter, "the streets and alleys of London. . .the. . .bur-
dened, whispering, emotional atmosphere of the monster town" (86).
"The sweep, the laborer, the sailor, the tradesman, even the dumb
beasts that render service or companionship, appeal to his kindly or
mirthful sensibilities and figure in his rhymes" (83). Hood shared this
London with his friend, Charles Dickens. Both artists were
influenced by the popular theater, and the poet's "modes of feeling"
and expression may be compared with those of the novelist: "Could
Dickens have written verse. . .it would have been marked by wit and
pathos like Hood's and by graphic, Doresque effects, that have grown
to be called melodramatic" (84). In a work like "The Bridge of Sighs,"
Hood is a poet capable of penetrating and revealing the
"tragedy. . .at the core of our modern life," and treating it with
"charity and forgiveness, the compassion of the Gospel itself"
(87–88).

One of Stedman's purposes in *Victorian Poets* is to find "illustrations of the poetic life" under modern conditions, and here he
emphasizes the difficult predicament of the professional poet who
lacks an independent income. Hood, as a magazine poet, journalist,
and editor could support himself only through "the most unremitting
toil." This had a deleterious effect on both his health and his
sensibility; "he gained the ear of the public not so much by humor as
by drollery, and joke he must, be the sallies wise or otherwise, or the
fire would go out on the hearth-stone" (81). Hood almost continually
faced poverty and suffered from ill-health. Nevertheless, this
suffering and journalistic experience, which "gave him closer
knowledge of the wants and emotions of the masses, and especially of
the populace in London's murky streets," made possible the poetic

successes of his last few years (83). Of course Stedman, who used the meter of Hood's "Miss Killmansegg" for his "The Diamond Wedding" and, like Hood, had the ability to write popular comic verse, refused to hazard the vulnerable life of the journalist-poet. But in a transparent reference to his own life, he tells the story of a writer of his acquaintance who "deliberately left the editoral profession" for an occupation "which bore no relation to letters," hoping thereby to have the leisure to write. But "as a businessman, with not the soundest health, and with his heart. . .not fully in his occupation, he found himself neither at ease in his means, nor able to gain sturdier hours for literature than vigorous journalist-authors filch from recreation and sleep" (81–82). The suffering of Hood, and his willingness to know the "wants and emotions" of the people themselves, made possible an artistic triumph denied to Stedman's more comfortable "acquaintance."

By way of contrast, the life of Procter, a happily married lawyer, was one of almost unrelieved domestic bliss and tranquility. Stoddard included an essay on Procter in his *Appleton's* series, and it is likely that his extravagantly high estimate of Procter's lyrics compelled Stedman to include Procter here. Of *English Songs* (1832), Stoddard wrote, "We question, indeed, whether all the early English poets ever produced so many and such beautiful songs as Barry Cornwall." According to Stoddard, Procter had achieved unrivaled popularity in America. The *English Songs*, he said, "hold the place they won at their first appearance, if not a higher one, and are more widely read to-day, particularly in America, than any productions of the kind which have seen the light in the present century."[53] While Stedman resisted this extravagant estimate, he still praised Procter's songs for their "spirit, alternately tender and blithesome. . .their unconscious grace, changeful as the artless and unexpected attitudes of a fair girl. . .their absolute musical quality and comprehensive range" (110). Both in its general outline and in certain of the details of treatment, the essay owes much to Stoddard. However, the writing lacks conviction, suggesting that Stedman was not so much motivated by genuine interest in his subject as the surreptitious desire to prove a point at the expense of Arnold. Fortunately, he was able to "confess" the error and make reparation in the "Supplement."

X   Mrs. Browning

It may be a surprise, even a shock, for the contemporary reader to find a separate chapter devoted to Mrs. Browning as one of the few

poets of genius capable of overcoming the restrictions of the period.
But when Stedman wrote, some thirteen years after her death in
Florence in 1861, the popularity of her poetry, enhanced by the
romantic legend of her life, had not diminished. Stedman himself was
drawn to the legend, and, while working on the essay, wrote to
Richard Watson Gilder, Holland's associate, "The paper on Mrs.
Browning I write *from the heart*, and really enjoy the work: owing to
the beautiful subject, it can scarcely fail to be popular."[54] He did not
approach the essay objectively, as simply the evaluation of a body of
verse; it was his "tribute to woman." The first paragraph establishes a
tone of tearful reverence:

There are some poets whom we picture to ourselves as surrounded with
aureolas; who are clothed in so pure an atmosphere that when we speak of
them,—though with a critical purpose and in this exacting age,—our
language must express that tender fealty which sanctity and exhaltation
compel from all mankind. We are not sure of our judgment: ordinary tests fail
us. . . . We do not see clearly, for often our eyes are blinded with tears;—we
love, we cherish, we revere. (114)

Still, the "critical purpose" is not entirely forgotten. Stedman
qualified the praise simply by calling her "the greatest of women
poets" (115). Indeed, there is truth in DeMille's statement that "Mrs.
Browning is rather severely handled."[55]
    We are dealing here with another aspect of the Genteel Tradition:
the poetry of men and women is placed in distinct compartments,
each with its own subject matter and standards. Men, as we saw in the
essay on Arnold, were expected to be objective, to separate
themselves from their work, to look "outward, not inward" (295). This
leaves the "inward," subjective field wide open for the ladies:

Most introspective poetry, in spite of Sidney's injunction, wearies us,
because it so often is the petty or morbid sentiment of natures little superior
to our own. Men have more conceit, with less tact, than women, and, as a
rule, when male poets write objectively they are on the safer side. But when
an impassioned woman, yearning to let the world share her poetic rapture or
grief, reveals the secrets of her burning heart, generations adore her,
literature is enriched, and grosser beings have glimpses of a purity with
which we invest our conceptions of disenthralled spirits in some ideal sphere.
(147–48)

Repressing subjective emotional experience in his own poetry,

Stedman was all the more ready to respond to it in the work of a woman like Mrs. Browning. He shared, with such writers as Tennyson, Kingsley, Ruskin, and Patmore, in the Victorian worship of woman. He found the best answer to the contemporary "woman question," the question of "woman's rights," in the speech of the Prince and Ida in Tennyson's *The Princess*: "For woman is not undeveloped man,/But diverse . . ." (167). "Diverse" in this context means morally superior; woman's function is to redeem man from his moral impurities. He quotes this line in reference to Mrs. Browning, whom he considers "the representative of her sex, in the Victorian era" (148).

Though thinking of the typical woman as "purer, more unselfish, more consecrated," than her masculine counterpart, Stedman did not, in an excursus on the "question of the artist's married life," recommend a chaste, bodiless existence for the female artist: "she should marry out of her own ideal, rather than not be married at all. So closely interwrought are her physical and spiritual existences, that otherwise the product of her genius may be little more than a beautiful fragment at the most" (135). Ideally, however, as in the case of the Brownings, marriage brings together partners who are intellectual equals: "there is no perfect love without mutual comprehension; at the best, a wearisome, unemotional forbearance takes its place" (134). And so he treats Mrs. Browning's marriage as the "chief event" of her life, giving her a "complete womanhood," and also enabling her to develop fully as an artist (132, 133).

In fact his treatment of the work produced before her marriage is particularly severe. Her art is "grossly defective," marred by "obsolete words," and producing "a grotesque effect." "Her slovenly elisions, indiscriminate mixture of old and new verbal inflections, eccentric rhymes, forced accents, wearisome repetition of favored words to a degree that almost implied poverty of thought . . . [are] an outrage" (126–27). But he sees a technical advance in the work produced after her marriage, due in part to her "stronger themes" and partly to the influence of Robert Browning. The two works that Stedman identifies as her "master-works"—*Casa Guidi Windows*, which contains the "Sonnets from the Portuguese" ("a portion of the finest subjective poetry of our literature") and *Aurora Leigh*—were written within the first ten years of her marriage. While Stedman's praise of the "Sonnets" is quite unbounded, his treatment of *Aurora Leigh* is discriminating. A "failure" when considered under the usual artistic standards, it is still one of the period's "representative and

original creations: representative in a versatile, kaleidoscopic pre-
sentment of modern life and issues; original, because the most
idiosyncratic of its author's poems" (140–41). Virginia Woolf has
argued that the poem deserves a reading precisely on these grounds.[56]

This essay certainly reveals the basis for much of the nineteenth
century reverence for Mrs. Browning as the most inspired of women
poets. But at the same time, in the sharp critical rigour with which it
exposes her artistic flaws, it also prepares the way for our rejection of
her.

XI   *Transatlantic Literary Relations*

In "The General Choir" (Chapters 7 and 8), Stedman attempts to
classify and review the work of 125 "younger or minor poets,"
including translators and hymnologists. He justifies this exercise by
asserting that it is only through such an analysis of minor poetry that
the critic can discover "the general tone and volume, at any epoch, of
a nation's poetic song" (234). On a practical level, he felt that these
chapters would enable the book to be used as a "guidebook" of value
"for uses of record and reference" as well as a critical document.
Clearly the attempt to achieve such breadth circumscribes the
chapter's critical value. He has space for only the most superficial
discussion of such figures as Clough, Meredith, and Christina
Rossetti.

Why, then, did Stedman attempt what impressed him as a frightful
task, one that filled him with "despair?" He once noted that visions of
the 125 odd volumes of verse waiting on his shelves to be read and
evaluated haunted his sleep.[57] But over the years he had made a
special effort to keep abreast of the work of younger poets writing in
English and, as he wrote to Edmund Gosse, "a good general
knowledge of this branch of my subject enabled me to attempt [the
essay] in the [limited] time and space given me."[58] He must have
sensed that the very process of examining contemporary English
poetry would reveal a new perspective on the current American
situation. Indeed, in concluding the essay he makes the seemingly
fatuous statement that "after a close examination of the minor poets of
Britain, during the last fifteen years, I have formed, most unexpectedly, the belief that an anthology could be culled from the
miscellaneous poetry of the United States equally lasting and
attractive with any selected from that of Great Britain" (291). No
longer need Americans accept colonial status, the humiliating
position of "children, guided by our elders, and taught to repeat

lispingly their antiquated and timorous words" (292). It may be that English poets will soon have to look to America for fresh inspiration, much as Americans have looked to the mother country for so long. The process of growing up and leaving home is never an easy one, and these comments do have an adolescent tone. But this awkward declaration of independence is really an attempt, a plea, for better literary relations between the two countries and to place them on a footing of equality. The extraordinary effort required to absorb, classify, and evaluate the work of some 125 "younger or minor poets," reflects the seriousness of Stedman's commitment to the process. And, despite the necessary limitations imposed by its scope, the essay, in its general characterizations and analyses of basic trends, is perceptive, and it did lead, on Stedman's part, to the opening of friendships with a number of English writers.

For instance, Austin Dobson, who respected Stedman's general treatment of society verse, began a correspondence with him at this time. Stedman wrote the introduction for Dobson's *Vignettes in Rhyme*, which, at his recommendation, Henry Holt published in 1880. Such was the popularity of this book that Stedman considered himself responsible for the consequent vogue of French forms in this country in the 1880s.[59] And it was with the opening of a correspondence with Stedman in December 1875 that Edmund Gosse "became extremely interested in establishing a literary reputation in the United States," something which Stedman did much to facilitate.[60] Of course, Stedman's most important friendship with the younger generation of English writers was with Swinburne. He also established relationships with such writers as Arthur O'Shaughnessey, Andrew Lang, Theodore Watts, Philip Marston, and others. *Victorian Poets*, in introducing a new generation of English poets to the American reading public, encouraged English writers to take an active interest in America. America represented a potentially lucrative market, and this may have encouraged Edmund Gosse to approach influential American authors and editors with special respect. But the tide was also moving in the other direction. *Scribner's* established a successful English edition in 1873, to be followed by *Harper's* in December 1880. During the nineties, Poultney Bigelow claimed, *Harper's* "had more circulation, even in England, than any English magazine."[61] The English public, which had long been interested in our major authors, became increasingly familiar, over the closing decades of the century, with contemporary American writers. In "American Books Abroad" Malcolm Cowley summarizes the report of one English observer who found in 1904 that "ten American books were being published in England where one had been published twenty years before."[62] Certainly Stedman, through *Victorian Poets*, and its companion, *Victorian Anthology* (1895), and through his close personal relationships with a variety of English writers, made important contributions to the productive "transatlantic dialogue" of the late nineteenth century.

CHAPTER 3

American Poetry: The Native Tradition

I A Divided Mind

STEDMAN'S decision to concentrate on criticism had by no means solved the old problem of vocation. Early in 1873 he moved with his family back to New York from the isolation of suburban New Jersey, where they had gone to economize. Withdrawing from business, he expected to devote his days to composition while taking part in the city's stimulating literary life in the evenings. But 1873 was a panic year—at one point the value of his seat on the Exchange plunged from $8,000 to $2,000—and, despite his best intentions, he found himself spending virtually full time in business during the first half of the year. As he explained to Taylor in December, literary society exacted its price:

Between you and me, a writer of any reputation in N.Y. nowadays, has a hard time to do any work—what with daily business, callers, correspondence, and the few tempting dinners, etc., which he don't wish to decline. As for amusements and general society, he must stoutly deny himself such recreation,—or meet the fate of Bret Harte and other victims of fame and favoritism. I came over here to renew my alliances and pick up my reputation; have partially succeeded in the latter, and have achieved the former with a vengeance! I *have* to furnish a *Scribner* paper every two months (at good pay, too,); and, having no time to write except from 9 to 12 P.M. on such evenings as I am free and *feel well enough*, I *don't* see how *Victorian Poets* can be ready for Osgood next Summer. . . . As for poetry, I haven't been able to write a line for 8 months—though my brain is again seething with rhythmic themes.[1]

It might well have been better for Stedman to remain in New Jersey, severely restrict his expenses, and devote all of his working energy to criticism and poetry. But he simply had to be in the "thick of things," and under the strain of writing *Victorian Poets*—he did not finish it until early 1875—the cracks in his fractured existence became painfully evident.

He recognized that he had reached the breaking point in February 1874. Having failed to complete his Tennyson article in time for scheduled publication in April, and unable to make any progress with it, he simply had to *"run away"* to preserve his sanity:

My brain is so *sore*, nowadays, that I can't get through my regular *work*. I can feel its *writhings and convolutions*, and at last am a little scared myself . . . [I] find myself too *nervous* to write it at all. . . . Christmas I had only $800. in the world; have since worked courageously in stocks, and made some thousands, and *can* leave. But the effort has been great. . . . I have no time to eat, sleep, or write.

He resolved to sail to Florida, where he was able to finish the essay. But again the effort was great; he vowed *"never again* [to] undertake a literary project that will force me to work when I don't feel like it."[2] He had to face the possibility that he simply was not capable of "sustained effort."

The next January, after finishing essays on Browning, Swinburne, and "Latter-Day Singers," and journalistic articles on his friends Whitelaw Reid (for the August *Scribner's*) and Charles Dudley Warner (for *Appleton's* for June 27), he suffered a serious breakdown. His doctor ordered him to take a complete rest at the Morristown home of his mother, who had returned from Italy in 1865. After a week or two, he recovered enough to complete the final essay, "The General Choir." But he was simply unable to go on, and had to have Robert Underwood Johnson, then a member of the *Scribner's* editorial staff, see the manuscript through the press. Completely exhausted, Stedman borrowed some money and took a long Caribbean vacation. Before leaving, he diagnosed his trouble, in a letter to Reid, as resulting from "anxiety and overwork."

Days when I don't read or write a line—now that I have closed up business—I find all the *bodily* trouble begins to leave me. . . .

I don't know whether its the stock-side of my head that's given way, or the book-side—but they don't trot together any longer. I make a living in Wall Street, but it is an incessant strain, and if I go back there next Fall, I shall run down again. Neither can I stand daily writing.[3]

So divided had his mind grown that he feared that the business side and the art side had neutralized each other, leaving him powerless to do anything at all.

Stedman thoroughly enjoyed the trip south, and responded to the tropical richness of the islands in a series of "Caribbean lyrics." But he found it difficult to relax for long. Early in April he grew depressed upon learning that he had missed a sudden turn in the stock market. He could only hope that if his health did improve he would yet "get some compensation for my terrible losses of time and money, and of the turn in the stock market. Shall go back to New York, nearly forty-two years old, and with all my fortune *yet to make*."[4] Although he may have realized intellectually years earlier that he would never "have money and health both," on a deeper level he still sought to earn the fortune that had been stolen from him.

After returning from the Caribbean late in the spring of 1875, Stedman reentered Wall Street. But far from accumulating a fortune, he steadily lost money. In March 1876 he borrowed $10,000 at seven percent from his wealthy uncle William E. Dodge just to stay in business. Over the next twelve months he earned $15,000, enabling him to support an "enormous living," pay his debts, help friends, such as an impoverished Henry Clapp, and subscribe a generous $30.00 to Whitman's *Centennial Edition of Leaves of Grass*. But, just as suddenly, his financial fortunes turned. He was victimized by what he termed, in his history of the New York Stock Exchange, the "peculiarly aggravating knavery" of a Mr. John Bonner, who "devoted his time largely to borrowing and lending money in the Stock Exchange, of which he was a member. Having rendered himself liable to indictment by rehypothecating the securities pledged with him by his fellow members and others, he disappeared, leaving balances of over $500,000 against him."[5] Once again Stedman was wiped out.

Wall Street, then, absorbed virtually all of Stedman's attention, leaving little time for literary projects. In November 1878, when he learned that Bayard Taylor had been mortally stricken, he felt his life crumble around him. But six months earlier Taylor had arrived in Germany to take up his ambassadorship. The appointment had been universally applauded: Taylor would be able to serve his country and at the same time devote himself to literature, particularly his long-projected biography of Goethe. That the leading figure of the "circle" had solved the problem of vocation had given hope to the others. But the news of Taylor's illness, which came to Stedman at a time of such trouble "that it seems as if the world, for us, were disintegrating," quickly destroyed this hope. As he confessed in his last letter to Taylor, he felt himself grow "mute and rigid."[6]

But Taylor's death in December 1878 gave Stedman the impetus to begin the "long-delayed" *Poets of America* by publishing an evaluative essay on Taylor himself in *Scribner's* for November 1879. Far from being the sort of puff that might have been expected, the essay is sharply critical, relating the manifold weaknesses of Taylor's art to the failure of a life that was "consecrated to poetry but not dedicated to it." Treating Taylor as a representative figure of his generation, the essay served Stedman as an exercise in self-analysis. Having confessed, as it were, his own weaknesses, he was now able to approach American poetry with a new objectivity and honesty. Paradoxically, Taylor's death led directly to Stedman's birth as a critic of American poetry.

II   *The Holland Age of Letters*

Poets of America is a consistent challenge to the accepted interpretation of the American poetic tradition, especially as the tradition had been defined by *Scribner's* powerful editor, Dr. Holland, whose influence "was so strong in the postbellum decade that one of his critics bitterly conceded that the period should be known as 'the Holland age of letters.'"[7] Immediately following the appearance of "Baynard Taylor" late in 1879, Stedman published sympathetic treatments of two "disreputable" poets, Poe, in *Scribner's* for May 1880, and Whitman, in November, giving a clear signal that he intended to undertake a radical revision of the canon. Recently, Holland had concluded "Our Garnered Names," written after the death of Bryant, with a vicious attack on these two poets.

Why an age which can produce such a poet as Bryant, who is as healthy and health-giving in every line as the winds that soar over his native hills, can be interested in the crazy products of a crazy mind [Poe], so far as to suppose that they have poetry in them, or any value whatever, except as studies in mental pathology, we cannot imagine. How an age that possesses a Longfellow and an appreciative ear for his melody can tolerate in the slightest degree the abominable dissonances of which Walt Whitman is the author, is one of the unsolved mysteries. There is a morbid love of the eccentric abroad in the country which, let us hope, will die out as the love of nastiness has died out. At present we say but little about our immortals, and give ourselves over to the discussion of claims of which our posterity will never hear, or of which they will only hear to wonder over, or to laugh at.[8]

Holland's list of acceptable and important writers included Cooper, Irving, Bryant, Longfellow, Whittier, Holmes, Lowell, Taylor, Stedman, Hawthorne, and Emerson. (Thoreau he also considered sick; Melville, of course, had been forgotten.) He praises this group for having produced an "American" body of literature distinguished by its purity: "Almost all the early literatures of other nations possess a gross, fleshly element, which is entirely lacking, and which would not be tolerated, in ours."[9] He insisted, then, that literature serve a moral purpose, that it "inculcate," as Benjamin T. Spencer summarized it, "the spirit and values of the purest civilization of all time—that of the Northern states."[10] Beauty is clearly subordinate to morality. And since Holland saw American literature as "the product of a branch of English culture," he insisted that the poet employ only the forms and metrical procedures of the English tradition. In *Poets of America*, Stedman takes issue with virtually every item of the Holland canon: Not only does he treat the "crazy" Poe and "dangerous" Whitman sympathetically, but he deflates the reputations of the sacrosanct New Englanders. He consistently attacks the "heresy of the didactic." While unwilling to concede with Whitman the obsolescence of the established forms, he accepts Whitman's stylistic innovations. Because of its service in leading the nation beyond the narrow moralism of the "Holland Age," this book is Stedman's most important contribution to American literature. It is also his best book.

III   *The First Cycle*

In the opening essay, "Early and Recent Conditions," published in August 1881, he formulates a concept of literary nationalism in the course of attacking the position of Richard Grant White, who was then "the most conspicuous proponent" of the view "that American literature must undeviatingly remain within the English orbit."[11] Unless Stedman could disprove this concept—so pervasive in nineteenth century American criticism—there would be little point in proceeding as he had planned. In a New York *Times* essay, to which Stedman refers, White had claimed that it is race, not milieu or moment, that determines a nation's literary expression: "It is impossible that a people mainly—and until of late as to the formative element, wholly—English in blood, English in speech, English in mental training and tradition, should produce anything but English literature—literature English in spirit, no matter what its subject."[12]

But Stedman points to the genuine diversity of the country's racial composition, involving "the traits of many lands and people."[13] Further, as a good Tainean, he insists that such factors as physical environment, history, republican institutions, and a unique cultural environment have all contributed to the formation of "a distinctive national character" (7). While the Anglophiles may think of themselves as essentially English, the English have a different perception of visiting Americans, who "are pronounced distinctively unEnglish and 'American,' however divided among themselves." Stedman insists, "the literary product of this new people differs from the literary product of the English, or any other people of the Old World, and I hope to make that difference clear in the course of these chapters" (6).

The major concern of the remainder of "Early and Recent Conditions" is to identify the factors that for so long had inhibited the growth of a true American poetry. Why did we have to wait until the second quarter of the nineteenth century for the simultaneous emergence of "many true poets?" The "special restrictions" include a colonial mentality, the fact that a people with advanced cultural and literary traditions settled a virgin continent, the leveling effects of democratic institutions, which initially retarded poetic growth, an understandable preoccupation with settlement and material progress, the lack of a paying market and of copyright protection (still a problem), and the failure to develop a true criticism. Such problems may not be obvious, but they were, nevertheless, "local and organic" and under "their serious pressure the rise of poetry was delayed" (26).

Since it is probably his best statement on the subject, I want to pay particular attention to Stedman's call for a new criticism, one which

applies both knowledge and self-knowledge to the test; which is penetrative and dexterous, but probes only to cure; which enters into the soul and purpose of a work, and considers every factor that makes it what it is;—the criticism which, above all, esteems it a cardinal sin to suffer a verdict to be tainted by private dislike, or by partisanship and the instinct of battle with an opposing clique or school. Such criticism is now essayed, but often is too much occupied with foreign or recondite subjects to search out and foster what is of worth among ourselves. (26)

Stedman himself had been guilty of critical "partisanship," most recently in a review of Taylor's last work, *Prince Deukalion*, for the *Atlantic*. His purpose, he wrote the dying author, was "to do as much as possible to excite interest, to insist upon the significant *first-class* nature of the work. Have criticized it just enough to show critical impartiality—such as carries dignity in the *Atlantic*."[14] Stedman's review, not listed in the bibliography in *Life and Letters*, appeared in the *Atlantic* for January 1879. In promoting, rather than objectively evaluating, the work, this essay reflects Stedman's identification with Taylor; to justify Taylor was to justify his own purposes. But the writing of "Bayard Taylor" had freed Stedman. He no longer had to take up the role of heroic defender of a besieged fortress; he had himself destroyed the fortress, making possible this call for a disinterested criticism.

The title of the next chapter, "The Growth of the American School," accurately reflects the organic basis of Stedman's criticism—organic in the broadest sense of interpreting the growth of American poetry within the context of the development of the national life. Specifically, he argues that American poetry has its true inception with the contemplative nature poetry of Bryant. He emphatically expresses his dislike for colonial poetry, calling the poets "simply third-rate British rhymesters, who copied the pedantry of the tamest period known," and their work "night,—utter night" (33). The time was not yet ripe for poetry. The best writing is to be found in the early chronicles, histories, and sermons. But for Stedman, literary nationalism is not a matter of adopting a program, and he attacks the "Pseudo-Americanism" of certain of the earlier New York and Philadelphia "literati" who sought to "create an indigenous American school. It was thought essential that purely American themes and incidents should be utilized. Cockney poets, emulating the method of Cooper, sent fancy ranging through the aboriginal forest, and wreaked their measures upon the supposititious Indian of that day" (42). Of the more recent poets—and Stedman discusses many—the work of only a few survives (and those in but a few lyrics): Freneau, Willis, Fitz-Green Halleck. Still "all this preliminary ferment. . .was in some way needful. The experiments of many who thought themselves called enabled the few who were chosen to find motives and occasions for work of real import" (44).

In explaining Bryant's position within the tradition, Stedman compares his aesthetic qualities with those of the landscape artists who make up "our first distinctive school" in painting: Cole, Durand, Kensett, and Inness. Most of these painters are identified with the "Hudson River School."

The literary counterpart of this school began with Bryant. . .the high-priest

of Nature in her elemental types. These he celebrated with the coolness and
breadth that were traits of the earlier painters named, though lacking the
freedom and detail of their successors. It is dangerous to measure one art by
another, or to confuse their terms; yet we feel that the relationship between
the pictures of Durand and Kensett, . . . and the meditative verse of
Bryant. . .is near and suggestive. (47)

This is an important insight for Bryant's poetry, as we shall see, but
even more important is its significance for a larger theory of American
literature. Since the country had been settled by people who brought
with them an advanced culture, literary development in the new
world could not follow the usual stages, from epic to historical and
patriotic works, to drama, and finally to lyric. It was only after the
"hardship and distrust of settlement" had been overcome and
civilization made secure that an indigenous art arose, first in
painting, then in poetry, to express "the adjustment of the people to
their locality" (46). In this case the natural process is reversed, and a
relatively advanced genre, the contemplative poem of nature,
became the country's first poetic form. And, as Stedman rightly
argues, the concern for nature is the "earliest and most constant" trait
of American poetry, uniting in an evolving tradition such poets as
Emerson, Whittier, Thoreau, Lowell, Taylor, and Whitman.

But having viewed the origin and growth of the tradition, Stedman
acknowledges that a cycle is over. The problems of modern
civilization, defined in *Victorian Poets*, have brought a temporary
halt to development. It is, then, an ideal time for a critic to attempt, as
Stedman is doing here, to review the first cycle of American poetry.
Criticism, too, has a place within the historical scheme.

Stedman is, as far as I know, the first American critic to apply the
organic idea, so pervasive in American literature and Romantic
critical theory, to the evolving traditions of the national literature as a
whole. It is an organicism complemented by the Tainean insight that
the critic must relate literature to its specific historical context. But it
was necessary for him to weld together these critical traditions if he
were to devise a theory to account for such seemingly diverse artists
as Longfellow and Whitman, Poe and Whittier.

IV *Bryant*

Certainly contemporary critics who wished to write objectively on
such figures as Bryant, Longfellow, Emerson, and Whittier faced an

unusual challenge. To the vast reading public, they were not simply literary artists, but secular sages. In a time of rapid and disturbing change, shabby materialism, and corrupt political leadership, these figures stood untouched, serene upholders of all that was best in the nation's traditions. Long before his death, as Stedman observed, Bryant had won an "incomparable" position: "He had become not only a representative citizen, journalist, poet, but the serene, transfigured ideal of a good and venerable man" (62). Could one evaluate his work objectively?

As we saw in his treatment of Landor, for Stedman the critic's proper business is with the work of art itself. But since many of his readers had already formed strong personal opinions—both positive and negative—regarding such figures as Poe, Longfellow, Whitman, and Whittier, he recognized that he must deal directly with the writer's public image. His relationship to the audience must be defined, its significance for the work gauged, and the relevant biographical facts established. But in every case, Stedman's strategy is to do this early, quickly, and with the purpose of directing attention away from the image and onto the work. In this way, he could write for both the general and sophisticated reader.

Here Stedman notes that Bryant, as an editor, has always been a strong, committed defender of liberty. But in analyzing the extraordinary public reverance for Bryant, he finds the shadowy hand of a hypocritical society. Bryant's social prominence as poet in "the wealth-respecting metropolis," would have been impossible if he had not also achieved "worldly success": "Even philistia has its aesthetic rituals and pagentry, and it was with a gracious and picturesque sense of the fitness of things that he bore his stately part in our festivals and processions" (64-65). But poetry is a "jealous mistress," and the business success that made possible his social position circumscribed his potential artistic achievement: "he did not give himself to poetry, but added poetry to his ordinary life and occupation. The reverse of this, only, can make the greatest poet" (75). Society, then, will have the poet only on its own terms—terms that may be destructive.

In dealing with the poetry itself, Stedman is quick to point out its limitations. He draws up a fairly comprehensive list, including such factors as a lack of "intellectual quickness and fertility," "stiffness," deficiencies of "passion, humor, and individuality," a diction that "when not confined to that Saxon English at everyman's use, is bald and didactic," a failure to change and develop, and a limited range

(69–71). Still, his purpose is neither to eulogize nor debunk, but to criticize, which, in this instance, demands the use of an historical perspective.

Stedman insists, "the fact must be kept in sight that he was the creature of our early period." A just appreciation of Bryant is possible only if the reader is able to recreate the situation at the time he began writing, when, "owing to an extreme precocity," "the eighteenth century notabilities on his father's shelves were still the approved models of style" (72). The key to Bryant's originality lies in his ability to develop, under the influence of Wordsworth, a style that enabled him to become a "meditative poet of nature." His range, of course, is narrow, and he used only two measures with real success, the iambic quatrain and blank verse, "the most difficult of all." But there is a compensating depth, an *"elemental quality* of his song," evident especially in his treatment of nature: "Like the bards of old, his spirit delights in fire, air, earth and water,—the apparent structures of the starry heavens, the mountain recesses, and the vasty deep. These he apostrophizes, but over them and within them he discerns and bows the knee to the omniscience of a protecting Father, a creative God. Poets, eminent in this wise, have been gifted always with *imagination*" (81). Though Bryant's art is limited to one note, it is one that he sounds deeply, and that has a vital historical significance. The aesthetic principles of his art are essentially comparable to those of our early landscape painters. Incidentally, several recent studies, most notably Donald Ringe's "Kindred Spirits: Bryant and Cole," have compared the work of Bryant and these painters.[15] Stedman anticipated these insights. This essay is a fine example both of the usefulness to the critic of comparisons between the literary work and the other arts and of the importance of the historical imagination.

V *Whittier*

"No one is less fashionable than John Greenleaf Whittier," Donald Hall wrote in 1960.[16] Today, despite a few fine essays and Robert Penn Warren's important *John Greenleaf Whittier's Poetry*, the poet is still neglected and out of fashion.[17] As a corrective Hall suggests, as had another New England poet, Winfield Townley Scott, that Whittier be approached as a regional poet: "The goodness of Whittier is tied to the deeply egalitarian, antityranical agrarianism of the small towns of New England. Industrialism, trade, and communications have conspired to destroy all traces of this society. Neither America nor American poetry has followed the way of thought that Whittier represented. . . .To read Whittier requires an effort of the historical imagination: we must learn to cope with goodness."[18] To see Whittier in this way is to establish him as a significant poet in his own right and as a forerunner of such later New Englanders as Robinson and Frost.

When Stedman wrote on Whittier in 1885, the situation was almost exactly reversed. More than fashionable, he was revered as "The Prophet Bard of America, poet of freedom, humanity, and religion; whose words of holy fire aroused the conscience of a guilty nation, and melted the fetters of the slaves." Stedman is quoting here from a tribute by Oliver Johnson, a founder of the New England Anti-Slavery Society and later a prominent New York journalist and reformer, but he confessed to his "own share of this feeling" (131). Nevertheless, the essay is balanced, "probably. . .the first critical treatment of Whittier from a strictly aesthetic point of view."[19] An exercise in discrimination and sorting out, Stedman's "Whittier," in exposing the weaknesses of the earlier propagandistic and pro-gramatically American phases of the poet's work, argues that he never wholly escaped the effects of his "technical carelessness." "Probably it occured somewhat late to the mind of this pure and duteous enthusiast that there is such a thing as duty to one's art, and that diffuseness, bad rhymes, and prosaic stanzas are alien to it. . . .A careless habit, once formed, made it hard for him to master the touch that renders a new poem by this or that expert a standard, and its appearance an event" (107). Still, Stedman ranks Whittier highly as "Distinctively the Poet of New England." Here, he is following the lead of the historian Francis Parkman, who wrote in a brief tribute prepared for Whittier's seventieth birthday, "John G. Whittier, the Poet of New England. His genius drew its nourishment from her soil; his pages are the mirror of her outward nature, and the strong utterance of her inward life" (97). Stedman quotes the statement in full, and his essay may be read as an extended comment on it.

Although a "literary nationalist," Stedman was suspicious of a too easy and too facile Americanism in letters. In responding to characterizations of Whittier as a "thoroughly American" poet, he asks, "Has there been a time, as yet, when any writer could be thoroughly American?" (96). In a sense, Stedman treats Whittier as an example of a "local color movement in poetry." Whittier's nationalism is a product of his faithfulness "to a characteristic portion of America,—the intense expression of its specific and governing ideas" (97). And as an authentic "bucolic poet of his own section," his work is different from such college-bred New Englanders as

Longfellow and Lowell. Here, he "surpasses all rivals. This is established chiefly by work that increased, after he reached middle age, with a consciousness of his lost youth" (115). Accordingly, Stedman calls *Snow-Bound* Whittier's masterpiece, in fact, probably the best of the modern idylls. In drawing up his list of Whittier's most successful works, he adds certain of the ballads, and such lyrics as "Telling the Bees," "Maud Miller," "My Playmate," and some of the religious verses. As with Bryant, Stedman does not claim for Whittier the status of major poet; he exposes and delineates the weaknesses and limitations clearly. But having done this, he is able, viewing Whittier historically, to see him as the authentic poet of a vanished New England and to identify the work that would survive.

VI *Emerson*

Stedman published "Ralph Waldo Emerson" in April 1883, a little less than a year after Emerson's death on April 27, 1882. The intervening period had witnessed such an extensive discussion of the various aspects of Emerson's "genius," that Stedman wondered if "anything new [could] be said of him" (133). But Stedman does have a new concept to add to the discussion: he challenges Emerson's assertion that "the true poet and the true philospher are one." In doing so he also, by implication, takes issue with a basic assumption of the more prominent recent estimates of Emerson, which had used Emerson's own categories to evaluate him. William Torrey Harris, the well-known Hegelian, writing in the *Atlantic*, had classified Emerson as a "poet-seer," one who "sees nature and history as expression of mind." Finding initial evidence of Emerson's seership in "The Sphinx," Harris asserts that "all his subsequent poems and prose essays repeat the same solution to the problem of life with new and varied forms. All nature and all history tell the story of incarnation of the divine."[20] Under this interpretation, poetry and philosophy perform essentially the same function.

Making a point that anticipates in some respects John Crowe Ransom's distinction between science and poetry, Stedman contrasts the methods of poet and philosopher. He did not, however, go so far as to allow for a possible conflict between the poem's "structure" and its "texture." Philosophy, in its concern for formulating abstract and comprehensive laws, searches for "pure identity; it follows Nature's trails to their common beginning. . .working back from infinite variety to the primal unity" (133). While the poet shares with the philosopher a concern for discovering and revealing "the soul of things," he proceeds in the opposite direction: "his poetry is an art that imitates Nature's own habit. He works from unity to countless results and formations" (133). Stedman emphasizes here the poet's unique ability to encompass the concrete in his work. Then, in his most important point, he claims that Emerson in his poetry did not consistently follow his own theory: "As a poet, Emerson found himself in a state, not of distraction, but often of indecision *between the methods of philosophy and art*. To bear this in mind is to account more readily for the peculiar beauties and deficiencies of his verse" (134).

The particular value of Emerson's poetry, then, is to be found not in its philosophical, but its lyrical qualities.

At times I think him the first of our lyric poets, his turns are so wild and unexpected; and he was never commonplace, even when writing for occasions. His verse changes unawares from a certain tension and angularity that were congenital, to an ethereal, unhampered freedom, the poetic soul in full glow, the inner music loosed and set at large. . . .If he sought first principles, he looked within himself for them, and thus portrays himself, not only the penetrative thinker, but the living man, the citizen, the New England villager, whose symbols are drawn from the actual woods and hills of a neighborhood. (150)

In this sense, Emerson continues and expands the American tradition of nature poetry—expands because Emerson, writing out of "an impassioned sense of [nature's] beauty," was not didactic. Stedman explicitly defends Emerson from Margaret Fuller's charges on this point.

But Stedman also recognizes that Emerson is not a complete poet, and brings two major charges. First, that his range is narrow: "Few have had Emerson's inward eye, but it is well that some have not been restricted to it" (156). And second, Emerson simply did not work hard enough to create well-integrated poetic wholes. Since Emerson was successful in finding appropriate forms for such poems as "The Problem," "Monadnock," and "Merlin," Stedman sees no reason why he should not have been similarly successful in all of his pieces. He regrets that Emerson did not compose more brief blank verse poems in the manner of "Days," which is "unmatched, outside of Landor, for compression and self-poise" (167). Both of these points are well taken. The second reflects one of Stedman's basic criticisms of New England poetry, its insistence on emphasizing truth of statement at the expense of aesthetic beauty: "The supreme poet will be not alone a seer, but also a persistent artist of the beautiful" (177). In the Poe essay, Stedman criticizes Poe for not giving appropriate recognition to truth in his poetic theory. As in *Victorian Poets*, he sought a balance between truth and beauty in poetry.

But if Emerson is not the complete poet, he has done much to prepare the way: His end was "not art, but the enfranchisement and stimulation of his people and his time" (137). In addition to his broad cultural role as liberator, he has been of particular value to poets, a point that is illustrated by the example of Walt Whitman. The "bardic" quality of Emerson's verse, found in a poem like "Merlin," inspired Whitman to encompass even "a broader liberty of song. . . . Emerson's 'Mithridates' . . . is at once the key-note and best defense of Whitman's untrammelled, all-heralding philosophy" (166). Stedman concludes with a prediction, which has been borne out, that whatever the limitations of his own poetry, Emerson will continue to hold a central position within the American tradition: "He chose the part of the forerunner and inspirer, and when the true poet shall come to America, it will be because such an one as Emerson has gone before him and prepared the way for his song, his vision, and his recognition" (179). By cutting through the great critical discussion on Emerson's philosophy, and taking issue with a basic point in his own literary theory, Stedman is able to find a way of evaluating Emerson's poetry and of defining his central role, as poet and theorist, in the American poetic tradition.

VII   *Longfellow*

"Nobody dreams of criticizing Longfellow from the point of view of 'mere literature': the human head and the human heart alike revolt from that," Van Wyck Brooks wrote in "Our Poets" (1915). He describes the thinness and superficiality of Longfellow's vision by referring to his "world" as that of a "German picture-book, never detaching itself from the softly colored pages."[21] But Brooks was hardly the first to find something wanting in Longfellow, and while he may have felt like a "prodigal son" for pointing it out in 1915, such guilt would have been unnecessary at the time of Longfellow's death in 1882. Writing in October 1883, Stedman observes that the poet's "admirers. . .no longer form a critical majority" (180). Indeed, in an 1874 letter George Boker reported to Taylor that Mrs. Stoddard had referred to that "weakling Longfellow, for whom no one can challenge more than a third class position, as compared to the mass of

English poets."[22] That Longfellow is a poet of decided limitations is one of the basic assumptions of this essay, and in defining the weaknesses of his work explicitly, it marks a definite change in public taste away from Dr. Holland's uncritical adulation.

But Stedman recognizes that the critical challenge is more complex than either attacking or defending. It is only after he has placed Longfellow's achievement within its proper historical perspective that he undertakes the job of critical evaluation.

He reminds those who think of Longfellow's poetry as "elementary" and who are preoccupied with discovering "new [metrical] modes," that just such an absorption and mastery of European styles as Longfellow achieved was essential before American poetry could find its own direction. Paradoxically, then, while he was "the least national of our poets," in several complex ways Longfellow helped make a national poetry possible in America:

He surely helped to quicken the New World sense of beauty, and to lead a movement which precedes the rise of a national school. . . . The apostolic nature of his mission. . .was religious, in the etymological sense of the word, the binding back of America to the Old World taste and imagination. Our true rise of Poetry may be dated from Longfellow's method of exciting an interest in it, as an expression of beauty. . . .Puritanism was opposed to beauty as a strange god, and to sentiment as an idle thing. Longfellow so adapted the beauty and sentiment of other lands to the convictions of his people, as to beguile their reason through the finer senses, and speedily to satisfy them that loveliness and righteousness may go together. (180–81)

Stedman supports his broad cultural generalization by recalling his own experience in youth in discovering Longfellow. He likens it to the rural child accustomed only to a "plain, colorless, rigid" village church coming upon the overwhelming spendour of a Gothic cathedral. The essence of the essay is in the sentence, "His verse. . .was like a pulsatory cord, sustaining our new-born ideality with nourishment from the mother-land, until it grew to vigor of its own" (182).

Stedman reminds his sophisticated readers of an additional point that must be kept in mind before proceeding to the actual criticism of his work; Longfellow's enormous popularity was based upon "his least poetic work,—verse whose easy lessons are adjusted to common needs. . . . He often taught, by choice, the primary class, and the upper form is slow to forget it" (190). Stedman's purpose in the essay is to demonstrate for the "upper form" that there is another Long-

fellow, while at the same time showing the beginners the limitations
of his popular, moralistic work. As we might expect, he attacks with
particular vehemence Longfellow's "moralizing," a "habit . . .
inbred . . . with the New England poets, most of whom have
preached too much in verse. He tacked a didactic moral . . . on many
a lovely poem" (215). The moralizing is related to an habitual attempt
to apply "his imagery in a formal way,—the very *ut . . . ita* of the
Latins, the *as . . . so* of the eighteenth century" (214–215). Only
those nature poems that are written directly out of his boyhood
memories of the sea are free of this fault. And he deals with the larger
limitations of his moral range: "there is something exasperating to
serious minds in his placid waiver of things grievous or distasteful"
(223).

Of course Stedman dismisses the early lyrics of uplift, like "Psalm
of Life." And in the main he is not sympathetic to the longer poems,
which he terms "pretentious." *Evangeline*, though a "little classic," is
flawed by the "sing-song" effects of the hexameters. The *Christus*
trilogy is a "disjointed failure," with only *The Golden Legend*
surviving. The poet's "works in dramatic form plainly represent the
craving of a versatile poet to win laurels in every province of his art."
The Tales of a Wayside Inn is "the semblance of a master effort, but in
fact a succession of minor ones" (208). What remains, then, is not the
domestic fireside poet, but the poet of imaginative ballads and several
lyrics of feeling. Among the ballads Stedman praises are "The
Skeleton in Armor," and "Sir Humphrey Gilbert." Longfellow's
strength is also found in such occasional pieces as "Hawthorne,"
"Bayard Taylor," and "The Warden of Cinque Ports." In such lyrics as
"The Fire of Drift-Wood," "The Lighthouse," "The Jewish Cemet-
ery," and "The Tide Rises, the Tide Falls," he "combined beauty with
feeling in lyrical trifles that rival those of Tennyson . . . and was
almost our earliest maker of verse that might be termed exquisite"
(191).

Stedman wrote at a time when Longfellow's extraordinary
popularity was being challenged by critical readers. And his own
essay, both in its influence on such younger critics as Woodberry and
Barrett Wendell, and through its broader cultural impact, certainly
hastened the process of deflating a reputation that could not be
supported. But the achievement of this essay is its ability to take the
discussion outside the realm of fashion by first considering the
historical value of Longfellow's work and then proceeding to make
critical judgements disinterestedly. As a result, Stedman is able to

find an important and enduring minor poet, a judgment shared by such later critics as Horace Gregory, Newton Arvin, and Howard Nemerov.

VIII   Poe: Avoiding the Biographical Fallacy

"Because of the extremes of admiration and detraction to which Poe's memory, as well as his life, has been exposed," the *Nation* observed, Stedman faced an even more difficult critical assignment in this essay, the second of the series, than in the first, on Bayard Taylor.[23] I have noted Dr. Holland's angry description of Poe's work, as "the crazy products of a crazy mind." One scholar has concluded, "the striking characteristic" of Poe criticism at this time was an "inability—to consider artistic matters without passing judgment also upon the personal failings which, largely through the initial instruction of Griswold, Poe was believed to have possessed"[24] Now Stedman does make comments that are critical of Poe's character. He avers that Poe suffered from an "inherent *lack of will*," preventing him from reaching his full potential (271). And he remarks that even "making every allowance, Poe was [himself] terribly blamable" for much of the difficulty of his life (269). But at the outset, he insists that all of this is simply beside the point; biographical judgments are one thing, critical evaluation quite another. Poe "was, after all, a man of like passions with ourselves,—one who, if weaker in his weaknesses than many, and stronger in his strength, may not have been so bad, nor yet so good, as one and another have painted him. . . .We are on firm ground with relation to his genuineness as a poet" (226,227). It is only his artistic genius that has provoked the extraordinary interest in his life, and, whatever his personal or aesthetic limitations, "he labored as an artist, and it is idle criticism which judges him upon any other ground" (263).

In evaluating Poe's "lyrical remains," Stedman notes how slender is the body of his verse. We have only a "few brief, occasional lyrics." After quoting Poe's own statement, that "Poetry has been with me a passion, not a purpose," he observes that Poe might well have composed a more significant body of work if it had also been a "purpose" with him. It is another variation on an oft-repeated observation in these pages; few nineteenth century American poets have fully committed themselves to poetry. Poe's "intellectual strength and rarest imagination" are to be found in his *Tales*. To them, and to literary criticism, his main labors were devoted (293,252).

In evaluating the poetry, Stedman begins with the popular "The Raven." Even George Parsons Lathrop, in the midst of a frenzied attack on Poe in *Scribner's*, had exempted it, along with "Ligeia," and the first of the "To Helen," poems, from his charge that all of Poe's work is the product of a "thoroughly unsound mind" and is "honeycombed with error and falsity, bad taste, undue outlay of language for small returns."[25] But addressing readers who can appreciate this poem, Stedman observes "how much more imaginative is such a poem as 'The City in the Sea'!" Then, as in the Bryant essay, he uses a comparison with painting to help elucidate basic aesthetic principles: "As a picture, this reminds us of Turner, and, again, of that sublime madman, John Martin" (242). His strategy is to point out to readers like Lathrop that they have missed the essential Poe, and then by comparing Poe's achievement with that of these painters, to suggest the depth and importance of this achievement. An art historian, Werner Hofmann, has provided an interesting commentary on this subject: "Threatened, and uncertain of his own creative power, man looks with fascination at the destructive power of nature. Artists. . .are drawn by the rages of nature, by her wild dynamic discharges. Pictures of rushing torrents and floods, such as those of Turner, Martin and Ensor, are just such responses to the call of chaos. They have their counterparts in the poems of Edgar Allen Poe."[26] Stedman praises particularly the artistic control that enabled Poe to write on themes of "sombre men and terror" so suggestively. The reader who persists in questioning Poe's mental state is asked to read "The Haunted Palace," which treats madness, "and see how sane, as an artist, he was that made it" (247). But Stedman's favorite among the poems is "Israfel," where Poe, "for once. . .got above the sepulchres and mists, even beyond the pale-faced moon, and visited the empyrean." The choice is based primarily on aesthetic considerations, "for pure music, for exaltion, and for its original, satisfying quality of rhythmic art" (248). Although he does not use the term, Stedman praises this work for approaching "pure poetry." Subject is less important than quality of treatment.

The central thesis of the essay is that Poe, "whether as poet or romancer," should be recognized as a "pioneer of the art of feeling in American literature" (263). Stedman, of course, continued Poe's critical battles against the notion that, in Dr. Holland's words, "In Art, as in Nature, Beauty has a subordinate mission."[27] But he criticizes Poe for a too exclusive devotion to beauty: "the question of 'moral' tendency concerned him not the least. He did not feel with

Keats that 'Beauty is truth, truth beauty,' and that a divine perfection may be reached by either road. This deficiency narrowed his range both as a poet and as a critic" (263). Stedman does not have room here for a full discussion of the complex philosophical and aesthetic issues raised in Poe's critical theory. But he insists that while Poe's exclusive concern for beauty may have been valuable historically in his attacks on the "mixture of sentimentalism, metaphysics, and morals" that characterized the literature of his day, it simply was too narrow to form a comprehensive aesthetic theory. But this, after all, is a minor reservation. Through this essay, which Jay B. Hubbell has called "much the best" written by an American critic on Poe in the "later nineteenth century," and through the scholarly edition of all of Poe's work (1895) which he edited with George Edward Woodberry, Stedman made a singular contribution to Poe criticism and scholarship.[28]

IX *Holmes*

The *Nation* succinctly summarized both the challenge and achievement of Stedman's "Oliver Wendell Holmes." "In attempting this critique Mr. Stedman faced unusual difficulties, for the place the venerable Autocrat fills is rather in the hearts than in the brains of his readers—in their kindly and truly social appreciation. His manner is that of talk, and criticism of it must always seem superfluous if not irrelevant. Mr. Stedman, however, has turned the corners cleverly enough."[29] "The first important literary critic to insist that Holmes's primary profession was not literature, but medicine," Stedman managed to identify the limitations of the verse without in any way detracting from the many-sided genius of its creator.[30] He "turned the corners" by responding to the Autocrat with a playful wit and sympathetic humor appropriate to a poet whose "distinctive gift" and unique "achievement" is that "in a field the most arduous and least attractive he should bear himself with such zest and fitness as to be numbered among poets, and should do honor to an office which they chiefly dread or mistrust, and which is little calculated to excite their inspiration" (290–91).

Treating Holmes as the most accomplished American practitioner of "familiar verse" or *verse de societe*, the essay is also concerned with defining the possibilities and pitfalls of a genre that was then very much in vogue. At its weakest, it is, as Stedman characterized much of the contemporary writing in the form, the idle expression that "a drawling society affects to patronize." But at its best, it is "picturesque, even dramatic, and [may] rise to a high degree of humor and of sage and tender thought." Such poetry "catches the secret of that day or this" (285). As W. H. Auden insisted, "Light verse can be serious."[31]

More than any other style, it is subject to the turns of fashion, and Holmes has been "in vogue and out of vogue" over the years (274). Just then, he was "warmly appreciated by verse-makers of the latest mode," who display "a new liking for the Georgian heroics and octosyllabics. . .queerly blended with our practice in the latest French forms" (275,276). Stedman, as we have seen, through his introduction to Dobson's *Vignettes in Rhyme* (1880), contributed to this vogue. (It is interesting to recall that about this same time, in Gardiner, Maine, Edwin Arlington Robinson, working under the tutelage of Dr. Allison T. Schumann, was mastering his craft through extensive practice in these forms.) However, while the current vogue represents an attempted revival, Holmes's work is a genuine "survival." "He wears the seal of 'that past Georgian day' by direct inheritance, not from the old time in England, but from that time in England's lettered colonies, whose inner sections still preserve the hereditary language and customs as they are scarcely to be found elsewhere." Even so, his work is distinguished by an "animation," a "courtesy and wit," and a "modern vivacity" wholly foreign to the "knee-buckle" period (275,276).

Accordingly, Stedman credits Holmes with a cultural role with which he was very much in sympathy: "dispenser of the ancestral gloom." Implicit in his light poetry is the wise recognition that "there is a time to laugh, that humor is quite as helpful a constituent of life as gravity or gloom. . . .that both fun and feeling are heightened when combined. . . .that pathos is an equal part of true humor; that sorrow is lightened by jest, and jest redeemed from coarseness by emotion" (277–78). While the great bulk of Holmes's verse is strictly occasional and will not survive, such poems as "Epilogue to the Breakfast-table Series," "At the Pantomime," "Dorothy-Q," "The Last Leaf," and "One-hoss Shay" deserve a permanent position. He is even better in certain of the "graver work," including "The Voiceless," "Avis," "Iris," "The Living Temple," and "The Chambered Nautilus." Such poems, along with the *Breakfast Table* series and certain of his other prose works, all did much to "relax the grimness of a Puritan constituency . . . [and] liberalize their clerical system" (295). All of his works reflect the stimulating personality of their author, a man for whom the "proper study is man, the regard of people and movements close at hand" (298). In this respect, as one scholar has observed, Stedman's "observation" that "Holmes by instinct and habit is a man rooted in the eighteenth century" would be "echoed in all future criticism."[32]

Stedman does not ignore Holmes's ingrained conservatism, which was at times responsible "for a very airy settlement of distracting social problems, to his own satisfaction and that of a generation of half-informed readers" (295). His primary loyalty, after all, was to his own "class"; he did not become "the avatar of new classes and conditions" (300). No easy or simplistic judgments are possible for such a figure, a man deeply rooted in the past, but one who helped to transform it; the "laureate" of Harvard and poet of Boston, who is also "a progressive and speculative figure" (300). In approaching Holmes in a playful yet respectful tone, Stedman precisely and sympathetically evaluates his achievement without making claims that the verse cannot support. Certainly, as Barry Menikoff observes, Stedman's treatment of the poetry is "sane and balanced."[33] It is also one of the best and most influential general essays on Holmes, wisely evaluating the poetry and demonstrating the importance of "light verse" within the American tradition.

X *Lowell*

Because of Lowell's strong influence on him in the postwar years, Stedman found it difficult to write an objective critical notice of his poetry. He and Bayard Taylor were angered when Stoddard published a review of *Under the Willows* (1869) in which their friend "frankly" expressed his opinion that "Lowell is a damned bad artist."[34] Stedman, choosing to publish his review of the volume in the *Evening Post* because the "*Post* background w'd please Lowell better & do him more good" than if it appeared in one of the magazines, explained to Taylor, "while I can't deny that Lowell is lazy and careless, & indeed hinted at it in my review, I am surprised that R.H.S. should shut his eyes, in the notice, to all his glorious points."[35] It goes without saying that if the reviewer is interested primarily in helping his subject and can do no more than "hint" at weakness, serious criticism is impossible. But one should not make the error of concluding that such timidity characterized Stedman's entire career. His major essay on Lowell, in keeping with his call for objective criticism, exposes the weaknesses of Lowell's art with damaging frankness, pointing to its many "technical blemishes," "verbosity," "moralizing," and failure of constructive power. Its impact was the stronger because it was clear that Stedman held no particular grudge, personal or ideological, against Lowell.

In fact, the tone of the essay is warm and appreciative. Lowell is "our representative man of letters," exemplifying "American culture at its best." With such prominent figures as "Marshall and Story, Pinckney, Wirt, Winthrop, Sumner and Bayard" he has done much to "advance the general grade of culture" (304–305). But to evaluate Lowell as a representative American, not as a poet, was itself damning. Indeed, Stedman asserts that when Lowell is judged strictly by his art, "as a poet in the end must be, he is one who might gain in revision and compression" (347).

At the heart of the problem is Lowell's moralizing habit, his distrust of beauty for its own sake. The art of "Rhoecus," for instance, is compromised by his insistence on treating the story "as an allegory conveying a lesson" (312). Such is Lowell's "dread of dilettanteism," that he feels compelled always to "express his conviction[s]" (312,314). In trying to do this while at the same time searching for a style, an artistic "method of his own," he "betrayed an irregular ear, and a voice rare in quality, but not wholly to be relied upon." The "eccentricities" of Lowell's style include faulty diction, "odd conceits, mixed metaphors, and licenses which as a critic he would not overlook in another." Such faults, as well as the failures in construction that one finds repeatedly in the poems, were certain to influence the "permanent value" of Lowell's verse. Stedman quotes Lowell against himself: "the work must surpass the material" (314–15). Most damaging of all, Stedman denies that Lowell may even be said to possess a style:

It has been said that Lowell's verse and prose are marked by a manner, rather than by style, in the modern sense,—which latter I take to be an airy, elusive perfection of language and syntax, that of itself wins the reader, and upon which writers of a new school have built up reputations. The thought, the purpose,—these are the main ends with Lowell, through prose or metre suffer for it, and there is no doubt that his manner exactly repeats his habit of mind; and so in this case, as ever, the style is again the man. My own explanation of things which annoy us in his loftier pieces is that his every-day genius is that of wit and humor. His familiar and satiric writings are consistent works of art. It is upon his serious and exalted moods that these things seem to intrude, like the whispering of the Black Man in the ears of a Puritan at prayers. (342–43).

This is of course damaging criticism, but Stedman did not intend to write a general attack. He tried to do justice to Lowell as "our most brilliant and learned critic." And in concluding, he asks the reader to think of his "high-water marks," which include "our best native idyl [the underrated "Nooning"], our best and most complete work in dialectic verse [*Biglow Papers*], and the noblest heroic ode that America has produced ["The Commemoration Ode"]—each and all ranking with the first of their kinds in English literature in modern time" (347–48).

There is evidence that while the essay angered Lowell, he privately acknowledged the truth of Stedman's negative criticism. Stedman visited Lowell in England shortly after the appearance of the article, and as is reflected in the following letter, had a memorable interview with him:[36]

American Exchange in Paris
35, Boulevard Des Capucines
Paris, May 31st 1882

Dear Mr. Lowell,

Looking in at this place for my letters, I chance upon a copy of the *Century*, and see that—after all—my recollection of the phrase used at the beginning of that article was pretty nearly correct. The idea I meant to convey was that, while your national reputation, & "representative" position, were not dependent *chiefly** upon your "exact" scholarship, that you were none the less a ripe and broad scholar, and *exact in those branches to which you have inclined*. In other words, I seem to have stated the case precisely as you stated it for yourself the other day.

Moreover, I want you to be so kind as to look at this article *synthetically*,—you already have brought your characteristic *analysis* to bear upon it. What is the general effect, the result, the summing up, of the whole matter? That is the important question. Nor could I so well defend the integrity of your general services and special gift as by freely acknowledging the few points which your adverse critics, as I thought, were justified in making—and which are quite incidental. I think I have long understood, & have indicated in this paper, how far you have been restricted or hampered by *circumstance*. Allowing for this, I try to show how your quality has made itself none the less evident, & how much you have accomplished in your day & generation.

But forgive me for alluding to your record as a poet & writer, & to my own inadequate but most sincere appreciation of its value. Let me rather say a word of sympathy, & of admiration, for you in your immediate perplexities. Your citation of the plaint made by Robt Lowe wd have gone to my heart, if its absolute want of application in your own case were not felt by me, and would not be felt by every man of sense and feeling. I suppose that every man, however successful, who has the sensitiveness which makes the poet, considers himself a "failure" at least once a day—generally in the bad fourth-hour before his boots are on in the morning. The truth is that your own career has been the one on which every young aspirant, in letters, has found his hopeless ideal: no writer so envied, so honored, among us all. Just now Tray Blanche and Sweetheart are yelping at an American poet and scholar who chances to have reached the foremost official rank. Of course you suffer, and will have yet more to endure, but—if they keep on—you will be made, in spite of yourself, a Senator or Governor. New England sometimes forgets her own—Massachusetts, *Never*.

> I am, with great respect,
> Most affectionately yrs.
> Edmund C. Stedman

*Professor Childs, Prof. Hadley, Whitney, et al.—for example—are known only as "scholars."

XI   *Whitman*

"Walt Whitman," Stedman's most important essay, appeared in *Scribner's* for November 1880. A strong defense of a writer of questionable repute, the essay's impact was profound. For here was a highly respected critic, and a respectable businessman to boot, insisting, in Dr. Holland's scrupulously edited magazine, that Whitman be recognized as "without doubt a poet of lyric and idyllic genius" (353). On three occasions in the past few years, Holland, the poet's most powerful and vehement antagonist during the seventies, had attacked him in his popular "Topics of the Time" column. He did his best to force Stedman to agree not to include an essay on Whitman in his *Scribner's* series, but Stedman was able to resist by threatening to withdraw the entire series from the magazine, forcing Holland to swallow a "bitter pill." It is ironic, then, that the essay that marked "the beginning of. . .public critical acceptance by others than the members of the Whitman circle," should appear in the only major monthly that refused his works and bitterly attacked him.[37] On the other hand, for Henry Mills Alden, the distinguished editor of *Scribner's* major competitor, *Harper's*, the essay led to a new appreciation of Whitman, as he explained to Stedman:

My first thought, after reading your paper was that I had underrated

Whitman. Seeing him on all sides as you presented him, my estimate was raised. It is the only essay on Whitman that has anything like completeness. It is not an easy thing to bring together within the compass of a maga[zine] article all that is essential to a fair judgment concerning a subject about which there is so much variance of opinion.[38]

Stedman helped "legitimize" Whitman, and his explanation of his stylistic innovations helped make him comprehensible.

To do this, Stedman had to go significantly beyond the terms of the contemporary debate. As the young Brander Matthews observed in a letter to Stedman, "Yours is almost the first saying about Whitman which has the great gift of common sense. It also has other qualities as uncommon as this. But this was what struck me. Other writing about him has generally been either supercilious or rhapsodic. Yours was criticism, cold, keen, and true."[39] The "supercilious" critics included Holland, E.K. Whipple, Bayard Taylor, the literary editors of the *Nation*, and Richard G. White, while the "rhapsodistic" came from such disciples as Dr. R.M. Bucke, Mrs. Gilchrist, William D. O'Connor, and John Burroughs. The rhapsodists seemed to demand that Whitman be revered as a prophet, as, in Bucke's words, "one of the greatest men, if not the very greatest man, the world has so far produced."[40] The detractors could be equally extreme. But as with Poe, Stedman transcended the biographical argument, concentrating on the work, not the man: "It is the fashion for many who reject Whitman's canticles to say: 'His poetry is good for nothing; but we like him as a man,' etc. To me, it seems that his song is more noteworthy than his life, in spite of his services in the hospitals during our civil war" (352–53). In demonstrating that one may form an objective estimate of Whitman's poetry without any reference to his personality or without preconceptions about the "legitimacy" of his verse techniques, the essay anticipates the approach of modern criticism.

The purpose of the brief biographical sketch that Stedman does draw is to "demythicize" the poet, to show that he is neither a vilified prophet nor a dangerous old man, but a working man of letters, facing, like all American writers, a difficult economic struggle. Citing the favorable review of the 1855 edition of *Leaves of Grass* in *Putnam's*, Emerson's famous letter, and the support of Whitman's associates, Stedman seeks to undercut the image of the persecuted poet, pointing out that "No poet, as a person, ever came more speedily within range of view" (359). And reporting on a survey of the editors of *Atlantic, Harper's, Galaxy,* and *Scribner's,* which he had undertaken privately, Stedman observes, "But little evidence was found of unfriendliness to him among the magazine-editors to whom our writers offer their wares" (361). Dr. Holland, as I have shown elsewhere, was the major exception. [41] While Stedman is somewhat too quick to dismiss the unique difficulties that Whitman faced, he may well be right in asserting, "what opposition the poet really incurred has done him no harm. The outcry led to plain speaking, and the press gave the fullest hearing to Whitman's friends" (361).

Here the broker Stedman gives an excellent "tip" to his readers. A footnote, which was not reprinted in *Poets of America,* reports, "Mr. Whitman's address is Camden, New Jersey. The two volumes [of the *Centennial Edition,* 1876] are sold by him for ten dollars. If book-collectors understood the quality of this limited edition, and how valuable it must become, the poet's heart would be cheered with so many orders that not a copy would be left on his shelves." [42] There is evidence that this "plug" was successful. William Sloane Kennedy wrote Stedman in December that Whitman told him that Stedman's "great kindness. . .in giving his address. . .has been the cause of quite a run on his home edition. He says this is all he has to get his bread and butter with." [43] Stedman's essay, then, was valuable to the poet in more ways than one.

The weakest portion of the essay is Stedman's criticism of Whitman's frank treatment of sex. Ostensibly judging Whitman by his own standard of fidelity to nature, Stedman charges him with violating the naturalistic ethos by portraying openly that which nature itself is careful to hide. "Nature is strong and rank, but not externally so. She, too, has her sweet and sacred sophistries, and the delight of Art is to heighten her beguilement, and, far from making her ranker than she is, to portray what she might be in ideal combinations. Nature, I say, covers her slime, her muck, her ruins, with garments that to us are beautiful" (368). In light of such an attitude, one can better understand Whitman's determination to resist those who implored him to publish an expurgated version of his works. Still, implicit in the essay as a whole is the idea that the "objectionable" passages were hardly so objectionable or dangerous that one should not read this poet.

Just as many of Stedman's contemporaries had been troubled by Whitman's open treatment of sex, so they objected to his apparent violation of the "rules" of metrics in poetry. Stedman argues that his metrical procedure is "not a new invention" but a recovery of "an old fashion, always selected for dithyrambic oracular outpourings,—that of the Hebrew lyrists and prophets, and their inspired English translators. . .and in recent times put to use by Blake, in the Prophetic Visions" (371). Stedman is broad-minded enough to accept both accentual and nonaccentual metrical procedures. Accordingly he denies Whitman's "primal indictment" of the "wanted forms" and of "form itself." Whitman himself, he correctly points out, well knows the value of "technique of *some kind*." Here Stedman feels called upon to defend the continued usefulness of accentual verse, particularly blank verse, "our noblest unrhymed form" (372,374). Resisting categorical judgments, he approaches the question pragmatically. Whitman's

present theory, like most theories which have reason, seems to be derived from experience: he has learned to discern the good and bad in his work, and has arrived at a rationale of it. He sees that he has been feeling after the irregular, various harmonies of nature, the anthem of the winds, the roll of the surges. . . . He tries to catch this "under-melody and rhythm." Here is an artistic motive, distinguishing his chainless dithyrambs from ordinary verse, somewhat as the new German music is distinguished from folk melody, and from the products of a preceding, especially the Italian, school. Here is not only reason, but a theoretical advance to a grade of art demanding extreme resources, because it affords the widest range of combination and effect. (375)

And he defends another controversial aspect of Whitman's style, the catalogues, by referring once again to the reader's actual experience. Here, Whitman appeals to "our synthetic vision." In looking through the window, we see "not only the framed landscape, but each tree and stone and living thing. His page must be seized with the eye, as the journalist reads a column at a glance, until successive 'types' and pages blend in the mind" (382). While Stedman does not offer a full explanation of Whitman's cataloguing, it is a perceptive start.

Having demonstrated the legitimacy of Whitman's poetry, Stedman then places him within the tradition of American nature poetry. Indeed, it is "as an assimilating poet of nature" that Whitman "seems to me to present his strongest claims." Apparently referring to a *Galaxy* essay by John Burroughs,[44] Stedman denies that Whitman is to be considered the "only" American poet of nature, but he recognizes something special in his treatment of man in nature,

Who else. . .has so true a hand or eye for the details, the sweep and color, of American landscape?

Furthermore, his intimacy with Nature is always subjective,—she furnishes the background for his self-portraiture and his images of men. None so apt as he to observe the panorama of life, to see the human figure. . .to hear not only "the bravuras of birds, bustle of growing wheat, gossip of flames, clack of sticks cooking my meals," but also "the sound I love, the sound of the human voice." (379–80)

The recognition of Whitman's "subjective" intimacy with landscape might profitably be compared with Josephine Miles's observation that "While for Blake, Keats, and others before Whitman, sublime figures were externalized, for Whitman and those after him they were internalized; earth felt through body, body through earth."[45] Stedman, in commentary on Whitman's technique, observes, "this is admirable, I say, and the true way to escape tradition" (380).

Stedman's "Walt Whitman," then, is far more than a long overdue "puff" for a neglected master. In locating Whitman's work within the immediate American tradition and the broader context of world literature, it both justifiies the poet and suggest a fruitful direction for further criticism. Its moderate tone led to the broadening of Whitman's reputation both among the middle classes for whom *Scribner's* was edited and the "literary establishment," as Alden's letter illustrates.[46]

XII   *Bayard Taylor*

The point to keep in mind about this essay—and Stedman stresses it at the outset—is that Taylor is not being considered because of the intrinsic worth of his poetry. On the contrary, as a poet Taylor was a failure, a case of arrested development. Stedman's main interest here is with the question of the artist's relationship to his literary situation. Taylor's career enables him to draw a portrait of the American poet living under recent conditions: "he furnishes examples of what to do—and what to avoid" (397). "Bayard Taylor" is a cautionary tale.

The moral is simple. In choosing to fulfill an ideal of a life rich in experience and of high social position, Taylor debarred himself from poetic creation of the first rank. The pattern is familiar: the precocious young artist makes a "brilliant" beginning, winning such dazzling success that he accepts the life offered to him by his audience, but in the process loses touch with the sources of his own creativity and fails to mature as an artist. Stedman argues that Taylor's artistic growth essentially ceased when he reached thirty, that with a few exceptions he never went much beyond such representative early poems as

"Hylas," "The Metempsychosis of the Pine," "Amram's Wooing," and the famous "Bedouin's Song."

His life was consecrated to poetry, yet not devoted to it. How much this means! Possibly he gained all the laurels he had a right to expect, under the conditions in which he acquiesced. To look further involved the surrender of immediate honors, of rare experience, of growth in various directions. It would have been strange indeed if, at his age, he had not accepted "the goods the gods provide,"—trusting, through strength and future occasion, to make even his half service of the muse as effective as the entire fealty of others who have won the crown. (409)

Taylor's trust that somehow his half-service would be justified was simply illusory.

Writing with the full weight of personal experience behind him, Stedman explores the implications of Taylor's actual choice, which involved the loss of "that subtler sense which, as no one knows more surely than the present writer, is so elusive, so often dulled or stunted by the force, the outcry, the perturbing conflicts of the social, the trading, the professional, or even the patriotic and political, world of action and toil" (409–10). Most importantly, the results of Taylor's choice are felt in his style:

He had the spontaneity of a born singer; but with it a facility that was dangerous indeed. His first draft was apt to be his best if not his only one. He had few affectations; his instinct being against obscurity and oddness of expression. He made his verse, as far as might be, the clear vehicle of his feeling. Of late years, in the desire to convey his deeper, more intellectual thought and conviction, he frequently became involved, and a metaphysical vagueness was apparent even in his lyrics. At such times critics thought his efforts strained, and his friends declared that he was not working in his best vein. (412)

There is pathos in the fact that Taylor's inability to solve the problem of his position as an American artist rendered him incapable of developing an effective style. Stedman, too, had a dangerous facility; he found it difficult to take pains. As Lowell observed in an early letter, "as one who has a sincere interest in you, will you pardon my saying that I fear you *improvise* a little too much? I have a fancy that long brooding is the only thing that will assure us whether our eggs are chalk or have a winged life hidden in them."[47]

Stedman related Taylor's inability to forge a style to his failure to maintain a vital relationship with either his immediate region or his country. His travel writing led him to search for new experiences all over the world, but there was a corresponding loss to his own poetry. There are in Taylor's work but a few exceptions to the pervasive stylistic anonymity: the "undervalued" *Home Pastorals*, and such ballads as "John Reid," and "The Quaker Widow." Yet Taylor himself "scarcely seemed to realize" the value of this work (412). Again, Stedman insists on "local color in poetry": "Authors are pretty sure to give us something of value when they render the feeling of localities to which they belong" (413) More specifically, "It was Taylor's good fortune, as a man who would live his life,—his ill fortune, it may be, as a poet,—to obtain the multiform experience for which his youth had longed. . . He cared most of all, in his heart of hearts, to be a poet, and he saw that, while going afar to invoke the Muse, he had given her the less chance to seek him" (414–15).

Especially when we consider the close personal relationship between Taylor and Stedman, this objective analysis of Taylor's weaknesses is a remarkable achievement. The *Nation* put the matter succinctly in commenting that Stedman "has reconciled frankness with delicacy, and friendship with a perspective which the judgment of later times will not find greatly in need of adjustment."[48]

XIII   *The Sonnet Men*

The concluding essay, "The Outlook," published as "The Twilight of the Poets" in the *Century* for September 1885, directly confronts the artistic failure of Stedman's own generation. At the time, Bryant, Longfellow, and Emerson were dead, and Holmes, Whittier, Whitman, and Lowell were old men, their best work long since done. No one, certainly not Stedman's close associates—already "veterans themselves"—had been able to provide fresh leadership. After a brief, intentionally uncritical survey of the work of such succeeding poets as Stoddard, Aldrich, Winter, Gilder, Lanier, and many others, Stedman concluded that it is impossible "to gloss over the dynamic insufficiency of our present metrical literature. . . . There is, if not a decadence, at least a poetic interregnum." Prose fiction has become the important genre; truly essential volumes of poetry were not being published (457).

While not pretending to excuse members of his own generation, Stedman analyzes the complex cultural and historical factors that have, undeniably, exerted a "distracting influence." The disturbing problems of modern civilization analyzed in *Victorian Poets* have become even more pronounced. Here Stedman considers the American factors, emphasizing in particular the Civil War, "a general absorbent at the crisis when a second group began to form." He touches gingerly on the relationship of his generation to "the favorite senior bards," who, following the war

were still in voice; their very longevity, fitting and beautiful as it was, restrained the zeal and postponed the opportunities of pupils who held them in honor. Our common and becoming reverence prevented both the younger writers and the people from suspecting that these veterans were running in grooves and supplying little new; finally, when this was realized, and there was a more open field, it became evident that the public was satiated with verse and craved a change . . . to some new form of imaginative literature. (437–38)

Stedman's analysis and condemnation of the current period is as acute and uncompromising as any that have followed. The numerous talented contemporary versifiers substitute "artifices and mere technique" for the "imaginative vitality" that is essential to true art. With the "instant vogue of novel forms, requiring adroitness for their perfection," we see "lyrics, sonnets, canzonets . . . produced on every hand. . . . Few . . . stand out boldly . . . it is questionable whether more sonnets, etc., are a real addition to [English poetry], and if a place worth having can be earned by polishing the countless facets of gems dependent on the fanciful analysis of love and other emotions" (459–60). No "brilliant leader" capable of breaking through this "intercalary" period by "devoting himself to the hazard of arduous and bravely ventured song" has appeared (461). Less than a decade later, in, ironically, a "Sonnet" published in The *Critic*, young Edwin Arlington Robinson also used the imagery of twilight to call, "Oh for a poet—for a beacon bright/To rift this changeless glimmer of dead gray."[49] Stedman's own terms for this period—"the twilight interval," "the interregnum"—have become our own.

As a way out, Stedman urged poets to take a lesson from the novelists, who "depict *Life* as it is, though rarely as yet in its intenser phases" (464). In calling for a more dramatic poetry, and, he hoped, a poetic drama, he confidently asserted that the author of such a poetry would be sure to receive a hearing. Poets should go beyond Whitman's depiction of "types" and study instead

individuals, men and women, various and real . . . in being and action,—in that mutual play upon one another's destinies which results from what we term the dramatic purport of life. Thus rising above mere introspection and analysis, poetry must be not so much a criticism as the objective portrayal and illumination of life itself—and that . . . upon the tides of circumstance where men are striving for intense sensations and continuous development. (466)

It is interesting to note that the work of Robinson, the first poet to escape the "twilight interval," is a dramatic poetry of "individuals, men and women, various and real." And Robinson joined such contemporaries as William Vaughn Moody, Ridgely Torrence, and Percy MacKaye in an effort at creating a poetic drama. I am not claiming here that Robinson or the others were directly influenced by Stedman, or that Robinson's aesthetic principles correspond to Stedman's. (One important difference is Robinson's insistence on confronting directly tragedy and suffering.) This was not his purpose. Although he felt that the "canons [of poetry] are not subject to change," he recognized the likelihood that the new poetry will "differ" from the old so that we "shall find it hard to accustom ourselves to the new" (476, 436). He was confident, nevertheless, that the young "will speedily interpret [their work] for us" (436–37).

At the end of the essay, Stedman directly faces the underlying question, Could poetry once again become a living art form? While poets busy themselves with beautiful trifles, the novelists are producing the significant imaginative works of the age. One had to face the possibility that poetry was simply an anachronism in the modern world. As we might expect, Stedman concluded the book with a confident assertion: the decline is only temporary; "the dawn" of a new era of poetic greatness "may soon break upon us unawares" (476).

CHAPTER 4

Between Poe and Emerson:
An Aesthetic Theory

I *His "Black Letter Day"*

THE *Nature and Elements of Poetry* (1892) is a book that Stedman had tried to avoid writing. In the introduction to *Poets of America*, written in September 1885, he declared his intention not to undertake another major book of criticism. "During the preparation of this work, the last of its kind that I shall publish, I have had my share of the ills from which none are quite exempt. It has been delayed by the rarity of intervals at which I could devote a wholesome energy to its completion, and feel assured that it would betray no tinge of personal discouragement."[1] The great "personal discouragement" during these years was the embezzlement of large sums from his firm by his elder son, Frederick Stuart, forcing him to make a temporary assignment of the business in August 1883. He helped Fred avoid indictment, but the entire affair, his "black-letter day," changed the course of his life. It would not be until his retirement from business with the sale of his stock exchange seat in 1900 that Stedman was able to pay off the large loans that he had secured to reenter business early in 1884. Even then he would be financially pressed until his death.

Even more difficult for Stedman to accept was the behaviour of his son. When in 1880 he had given Fred a partnership in his firm, the business was prospering. In the first five months of 1879, Stedman had earned $11,000 above living expenses, enabling him to spend a delightful summer in England. And after Fred joined the firm, E. C. Stedman and Co. Bankers and Brokers enjoyed phenomenal success. Operating from tastefully furnished offices at 36 Broadway, the partners accumulated some $200,000 over the next few years. The senior partner, who had purchased a fine home on West Fifty-fourth Street in 1879, was encouraged in 1883 to begin construction of "Kelp Rock," an imposing stone "cottage" on New Castle Island, off the

103

New Hampshire shore. He was vacationing with T. B. Aldrich in New Hampshire in August of 1883 when a "strangely disturbed" letter from Fred prompted him to return to New York.

He quickly discovered that his son had been deceiving him by using securities held by the firm as collateral for his own reckless and confused speculations, carried on secretly with another firm, Cecil Ward and Co. Now the losses somehow had to be made up. Deluged with offers of loans, Stedman might have remained in business. But the pressure of the situation was such that he placed the firm in receivership and withdrew from the street.

Renting his New York home at a good price, Stedman found that this rental income, along with his earnings from essays and poetry, would be enough to support a modest existence. But he had worn the broker's collar too long. Once again citing the value of his seat as a life insurance policy, he reentered business in January. He refused to walk away from a ruined business, nor would he allow those who had entrusted their funds to him to suffer through the dishonesty of his son. Of course this meant that he would have to assume heavy debts. And at this time, work had progressed far enough on the eleven volume *A Library of American Literature* (1889–90) that he realized how demanding this project would prove to be. We can understand, then, why Stedman, in completing *Poets of America*, would seek to reassure himself that he would not have to face another demanding critical volume.

II   *The Battle of Genres*

Stedman was immediately drawn into the critical fray when W. D. Howells, in reviewing *Poets of America* in his prominent "Editor's Study" column for *Harper's* (March 1886), questioned poetry's very right to survival. The general tone of the review is friendly, Howells praises the essays on the major American poets unreservedly, noting that Stedman's is a "singularly judicial" criticism, "which, indeed, we could not praise too highly." But he takes sharp issue with two related points, the very existence of "genius," a quality that is basic to Stedman's aesthetic theory, and the prediction of a revival of American poetry.[2] Implicit in this attack are certain of the essential features of the theory of "Critical Realism" that he was formulating during the years he wrote the "Editor's Study," 1885–1891.

Of the lack of interest in poetry he gives humorous and telling confirmation. Recalling the days when "every quarterly, monthly, weekly, had its gridiron well heated, and its tender young poet or poetess always grilling over the coals for the amusement of the spectators," he asks, "But what journal now keeps a hot gridiron, or broils bards of any sex or age?" Society no longer felt it necessary to defend itself against the poet. But Howells then turns his gentle humor in the direction of serious satire by questioning the very desirability of a poetic revival:

> If . . . we are at the end of our great poets for the present, we do not know that we shall altogether despair. There are black moments when, honestly between ourselves and the reader, the spectacle of any mature lady or gentleman proposing to put his or her thoughts and feelings into rhymes affects us much as the sight of some respected person might if we met him jigging or caracoling down the street, instead of modestly walking. . . . hasn't there perhaps been enough [poetry]?[3]

This attack is obviously aimed in the first instance at the rapidly proliferating numbers of versifiers who were turning out quantities of what may most charitably be termed subliterary verse. But it is also directed at the very concept of poetic inspiration.

Howells was concerned during these years with defining a democratic American art, one that would foster a broad social coherence: "The real sentiment of to-day requires that the novelist shall portray a section of real life, that has in it a useful and animating purpose. All the good work of our times is being done on this theory."[4] In responding to Stedman's obtuse, if not insulting, suggestion in *Poets of America* that writers such as Howells, who had produced promising poetry early in their careers, were now concentrating on prose fiction because of the greater financial rewards, Howells insisted on the primacy of the novel: "If practicable, [the young writer] ought to believe that to write the great possible novel is to surpass all make and manner of versing whatsoever, hitherto accomplished or imagined."[5]

Howells is not calling for the objective portrayal of the real life around him, for "absolute realism." The study of "real life," he was confident, would in fact reveal a "useful and animating purpose." The expectation that art serve an animating purpose seems to me to be a quieter way of asking art to serve the traditional function of inspiration. "In fact, many early American realists," as one scholar has noted, felt justified in incorporating into their work inspirational purposes by the assumption "that evolution implied a moral teleology. If for the purposes of fiction some foreshortening was

necessary, if good triumphed sooner than it might in life, the final
pattern of the story was nonetheless true to the greater scheme of
things."[6] As we will see, Stedman too built his position around moral
teleology, which, he claimed, was justified by evolutionary theory.
Accordingly, since the leading realists, such as Howells and Hamlin
Garland, were meliorists, it is inaccurate to speak of a sharp,
unbridgeable cleavage between "realists" and "idealists."

Howells' criticism of Stedman's concept of genius is directly
relevant to an important question in the critical debate, the
expression of personality in art. He found the idea that certain
individuals had been granted powers of perception and expression
beyond the reach of the most hard-working citizens anathema to his
democratic instincts. The theory of genius, he argued, is "wholly
opposed to the spirit of free institutions and the principles of civil
service reform."[7] In the modern democracy the artist is a craftsman
who should strive to bring about that "human equality of which the
instinct has been divinely implanted in the human soul."[8] Genius,
then, is nothing more than "the *Mastery* which comes to any man
according to his powers and diligence in any direction, conscious or
unconscious, nature has given him."[9]

The realists variously labeled their opponents as idealists or
romanticists. They personified the romantic frame of mind in the
image of the "unreconstructed Southerner: a hot-headed, effusively
courteous adventurer, somewhat too handy with the ladies" and in
the image of the Northern Robber Baron.[10] Truthful, sober images of
common reality were needed to assist the people in understanding
the dangers posed by emotional excesses. As Clara and Rudolph Kirk
have pointed out, "Howells never misses a chance to inveigh against
the noble attitudes which his characters assume."[11] For this
movement toward sobriety, poetry, inextricably linked with the
romantic expression of individual emotions, became suspect.

Stedman replied to Howells immediately, in "Genius," published
in the distinguished but failing the *New Princeton Review* for
September 1886. Identifying the true poet as a genius, Stedman
endows him with specifically religious powers: Genius is a quality
"*inborn*, not alone with respect to bodily dexterity and the fabric of
the brain, but as appertaining to the power and bent of the soul
itself."[12] Stedman bases his assertions on two separate arguments,
historical and analytical. The former traces the ancestry of the
concept and shows its wide acceptance through history by the best
minds, from Plato to recent Americans. The analytical argument

relies heavily on "the most penetrative of modern thinkers," Schopenhauer and von Hartmann, who have subjected the concept "to the test of a stern and ruthless philosophy." Even after his rigorous analyses, however, Schopenhauer is able to assert that "the intellect [of the genius] is of greatest purity, and becomes *the true mirror of the world*. . . . In such moments, as it were, the soul of immortal works is begotten."[13] Here Stedman is in a familiar position for a nineteenth century American: following a German philosopher in an argument seeking to establish the identity of the human soul with nature, which becomes in this tradition an expression of the divine. In his own summarizing definition, "genius lies in the doing of one thing, or many things, through power resulting from the unconscious action of the free intellect, in a manner unattainable by the conscious effort of ordinary men."[14] Stedman considered such a concept of genius essential if he were to justify an art of prophetic insight and power, an art that did more than encompass common reality, common beauty.

Nevertheless, in the conclusion of the essay, he seeks to secure a common ground between "idealists" and romanticists, on the one hand, and the realists. Recognizing that virtually all of the significant work of the age was being done in prose fiction, he calls upon the poet to learn from the novelist and put more truth, more "reason in his rhymes." At the same time, he argues that the novelist might profitably emulate "the color and passion of the poet."[15] His essential contention is that it is possible for the poet to remain true to the life around him without surrendering his poetic heritage.

III   *The Nature and Elements of Poetry*

Stedman recognized that his essay on "genius" was hardly adequate either as a response to Howells or as a statement of the function of poetry in the contemporary world. But he was preoccupied during the next few years with completing the *Library*. Late in 1889 he was saddened by his inability to accept an invitation from Johns Hopkins University to inaugurate the newly endowed Turnbull lectureship in poetry. Work on the *Library*, as well as "private troubles," he explained to the Hopkins officials, "have so exhausted me that the physicians forbid me to accept any new engagements. They prescribe that unattainable thing—a year of 'absolute rest.' "[16] But when asked to reconsider and offered a year's extension, he simply had to accept. He felt that the establishment of such a lectureship at a great scientific university like Hopkins was itself a sign that poetry had a central role to play in the new scientific age. The chair at Oxford was the only other such lectureship devoted entirely to poetry at an English-speaking university. And he had been concerned that with the introduction in America of graduate literary studies based on Germanic methods, the quality of the teaching of literature had declined in American colleges and universities. "The whole trend of our College policy has been toward scholastic analysis, philology, etc., and scornful of ideality and generalization," he wrote Charles Richardson. [17] But most importantly, the course of eight lectures on poetry presented a splendid opportunity to put the entire realist-romanticist controversy into proper perspective.

It was only after accepting the invitation that Stedman learned, in the public announcement of the series, that the honor of inaugurating the lectureship had originally been tendered to Lowell, who had been forced to refuse because of ill health. But Lowell's withdrawal—he was to die in August 1891—emphasized a fact that could no longer be denied: the nation's leadership had changed. Howells in fiction and Stedman in poetry were the leading critics, and both lived in New York City. Especially at a time when the future of poetry was in doubt, Stedman was not one to shirk the responsibilities of leadership and, explaining his "reconsideration" of his stated intention not to undertake another critical volume, observed, "under stress of public neglect or distaste, the lovers of any cause or art find their regard for it more unshaken than ever." [18] Stedman could not resist, then, casting himself in the role of heroic defender of a besieged fortress. The well-publicized lectures were delivered in Baltimore in the spring of 1891, repeated the next year at Columbia and the University of Pennsylvania, published in the *Century*, and brought out in book form by Houghton Mifflin.

In hindsight, the debate between Howells and Stedman over the future of poetry may strike us as foolish. It certainly was unnecessary for Howells, as part of his advocacy of realism, to carry his argument to the point of claiming that poetry had outlived its usefulness. Perhaps he was twitting his friend. But Stedman responded on Howells' terms. Even while admitting that poetry is moribund and that the significant literary work was now being done in prose fiction, he cannot help but argue for its ultimate primacy; poetry "is still the most vital form of human expression" (43), the "most ideal and comprehensive of those arts which intensify life and suggest life's highest possibilities" (5).

A more temperate, a broader critic may well have seen the need for an aesthetic statement that would not only defend poetry but also encompass the other genres. Stedman's remarks at the conclusion of "Genius" show that he did recognize that both poet and novelist have important work to do. And in the fourth chapter of *The Nature and Elements of Poetry*, he comments sensibly on the great contemporary debate "concerning realism and romanticism, of late so tediously bruited." While such discussions may have a limited stimulative value, in the end they miss the essential question: "How good is each in its kind? How striking is the gift of him who works in either fashion? Genius will inevitably find its own fashion, and as inevitably pursue it" (145). The critic cannot be dogmatic; he cannot reject a work simply because it does not belong to a particular school or mode or genre. Stedman's explicit treatment of this subject should help dispel the general notion that he was an unreasoning antagonist of realistic fiction, a sworn foe of the ordained movements of his time. But for *The Nature and Elements* as a whole, he is led to adopt the self-defeating strategy of defending poetry by stressing just those elements that differentiate it from prose fiction. The result is an unsupportably grand view of the poet and his function.

In concluding his introduction to *Nature and Elements*, Stedman asserts that the principles formulated here are entirely consistent with those that had guided his practical criticism and suggests that the present volume could well serve as "a natural complement" to the earlier two. There are, however, differences of emphasis and tone, of commission and omission, which require special attention. This is due in the first instance to the constraints of aesthetic theorizing itself—at least as practiced by Stedman. In his "practical" work, his primary concern had been the poem itself; with a few notable exceptions, such as his initial evaluations of Browning and Arnold, he did not impose theoretical judgments on individual works but allowed the works themselves to suggest broader theories. But as a theoretician, Stedman does not allow himself such flexibility; he is primarily concerned with formulating general rules, and the citations of individual works, drawn from the whole range of Western poetry from Homer and the Bible to Browning and Whitman, are made to fit the principle. Further, in the practical criticism, Stedman had operated in the historical dimension, respecting the limitations exacted, and the opportunities extended, by the accidents of time and place. As in his treatment of Whittier and Taylor, he emphasized the importance for the artist of being true to his own environment. Here, however, in attempting to convince his audience of the transcendent value of poetry, Stedman formulates an aesthetic that celebrates how poetry might ideally work. He makes demands of his "ideal" poet that could not be made of any individual artist.

Now Stedman gives primary importance to the poet's role as truth-seeker. Throughout his criticism, as we have seen, he had maintained that poetry is an art devoted equally to truth and beauty, and here he does assert that "in the last reduction," truth and beauty are "equivalent terms, and beauty is the unveiled shining countenance of truth" (187). But in *Victorian Poets* and *Poets of America*, in attacking the pervasive moralism so vigorously expounded by his own editor, Dr. Holland, he had insisted on the recognition of beauty: his major contribution to the critical debate of the 1870's and 1880's had been to right a balance that had existed in favor of the didactic. But now, when the old French forms were all the rage and poetry lacked a vital purpose, Stedman felt a new emphasis on truth and content was essential. In the first chapter, "Oracles Old and New," a historical review of important definitions of poetry, Stedman concentrates on such theorists as Plato, Sidney, Coleridge and Shelley who testify to poetry as a creative, prophetic, impassioned, and imaginative form. The poet's function is not simply to imitate that which exists, to recreate his immediate experiences, but to reveal a higher vision, a higher truth. In placing himself firmly within the Platonic tradition, Stedman recognizes not Poe but Emerson, "our seer of seers," as the prototypical American theorist: the transcendentalist "creed," "with its inclusion of the bard as the revealer of the secret of things," while not a complete statement, "lays stress upon [poetry's] highest attribute," the revelation of spiritual truth (24).

Expanding upon the statement of Wordsworth and Coleridge that poetry is the "antithesis of science," Stedman identifies its two unique functions, to recreate the physical world as it is "known to eye, ear, and touch," and to discover the governing ideas behind things. Under the second function, the poet exercises "an insight which pierces to spiritual actualities, to the meaning of phenomena, and to the relations of all this scientific knowledge" (28). Here Stedman emphasizes the second, the poetry of ideas at the expense of the first, a poetry of things.

In *Victorian Poets* and *Poets of America* Stedman had blamed the disturbances caused by the new scientific ideas for the recent decline of poetry. Then he could do no more than predict an ultimate reconciliation. But now, inspired by evolutionary theory and recent scientific and technological progress, he confidently, even explicitly, foretells it: "Theology, teaching immortality, now finds science deducing the progressive existence of the soul as an inference from the law of evolution. Poetry finds science offering it fresh discovery as the terrace from which to essay new flights" (37). Such a reconciliation of poetry and science would justify a new concern for philosophical ideas in poetry, and Stedman attempts to demonstrate that his ideal poet would leave Howells' novelist, commanded to imitate common reality, far behind. But clearly, Stedman slights the first, and we might say, the most important function of the poet—recreating the actual physical world. In reaction to such philosophical positions as Stedman's, the Imagists would assert the primacy of the physical world: "No meaning except in things." But the excitable Stedman found it impossible to resist his new vision: "For beyond both the phantasmal look of things and full scientific attainment there is a universal coherence—there are infinite meanings—which the poet has the gift to see, and by the revelation and prophecy of which he illumines whatever is cognizable" (33).

This is not to say that Stedman here is rejecting the tradition of Poe. He continues his attack on the didacticism of the Transcendentalists, asserting that "carried too far, the Platonic idea often has vitiated the work of those minor transcendentalists who reduce their poetics to didactics" (24). His formal definition that poetry is *"rhythmical, imaginative language, expressing the invention, taste, thought, passion, and insight, of the human soul,"* is confessedly based on Poe's statement that poetry is "the *Rhythmical* Creation of Beauty" (44). Indeed, George DeMille has pointed to this similarity in support of his charge that *"The Nature and Elements of Poetry* is nothing more nor less than *The Poetic Principle* and *The Rationale of Verse*, enormously expanded in expression, profusely illustrated by quotations from poets ancient and modern, with a few errors removed, and a few sharp edges filed off." [19] Howard Mumford Jones has summarily dismissed this charge of "intellectual dishonesty," but it will be useful, as a means of clarifying Stedman's position, to consider the question further. [20]

The important point is that Stedman both acknowledges his debt to Poe and explicitly defines his differences from him. He comments, for instance, that "one need not accept [Poe's definition] as a sufficient statement, but one may assert that no statement is sufficient which does not pointedly include it" (152). He modifies Poe's statement by adding to it the idea that poetry must also have significant content, pointing out that poetry "so depends on the

elements of emotions and truth that when these are not expressed
. . . you may suspect the beauty to be defective and your sense of it
mistaken" (168). Again he asserts, "All in all, if concrete beauty is not
the greatest thing in poetry, it is the one thing indispensible, and
therefore we give it earliest consideration" (167–68). As indispensi-
able as "concrete beauty" is, it is not its most important, its greatest,
element, and Stedman bases this defense primarily on poetry's
prophetic powers.

While Stedman's emphasis on ideas in poetry marks *The Nature
and Elements of Poetry* as a typically Victorian work, his reconsideration of the question of the expression of personality in poetry
anticipates modern approaches. We have seen that throughout his
career, Stedman had given strong preference to the objective in art,
to what he calls here the "Not Me." In his own poetry, he had, for the
most part, avoided the subjective. In the third chapter, "Creation
and Self-Expression," an historic review of great objective poetry, he
still terms such work intrinsically superior: "That which is impersonal, and so very great at its best, appears the more creative as being
a statement of things discerned by free and absolute vision. The
other order is so affected by relations with the maker's traits and tastes
that it betokens a relative and conditioned imagination" (77). But he
wisely recognizes that objective work, great as it may be, is simply
impossible in the modern world. Much as Matthew Arnold may have
longed to create an objective masterpiece as a way of escaping the
spiritual unrest that is a natural function of the heightened
self-consciousness of the modern world, such creation is impossible.
Arnold's best work is not his imitative "classical" dramas, but his
subjective lyrics. The question, then, is not whether personality is to
be expressed in modern poetry, but how it can best be expressed. As
would the great modernists Yeats, Pound, and Eliot after him,
Stedman looks back to Dante's *Divine Comedy* as a model: "his epic
declares the intense personality that must have voice; not merely
expression of the emotion that inspired his minor numbers. . .but
also his insight concerning the master forces of human life and faith
and the historic turmoil of his era" (113).

In the fourth chapter, "Melancholia," Stedman defines the
characteristic modern note as one of sadness and grief, of Dürer's
"Melancholia." The modern artist recognizes that "it is better to
suffer than to lose the power of suffering" (143). Responding to those
who sought totally objective art, he asserts that poetry should not be
judged

by its degree of objectivity. Our inquiry concerns the poet's inspiration, his production of beauty in sound and sense, his imagination, passion, insight, thought, motive. Impersonal work may be never so correct, and yet tame and ineffective. . . .Where the nature of the singer is noble, his inner life superior to that of other men, the more he gives us of it the more deeply we are moved. We suffer with him; he makes us sharers of his own joy. In any case the value of the poem lies in the credentials of the poet. (144–45)

Stedman is not insisting that art serve an explicitly moral purpose, but that on the highest plane aesthetic and moral considerations merge.

His treatment of "beauty" is also flexible. He recognizes that the same aesthetic standards cannot properly be applied to the art of all countries and periods (164). And he comes close to a complete acceptance of the organicism so important to American aesthetic theory: "That beauty does go somewhat with use is plain from its creation by necessity. . . .If the essence of beauty lies in conformity to the law and fitness of things, then all natural things are as beautiful as they can be,—that is, beauty is their natural quality" (156). But he finally pulls back from a complete affirmation of a relative or functionalist position, asserting that all peoples recognize "an extra-mundane conception of beauty, founded in the spirit of man, and this again conforms itself to the spirit of each race. Through it the poets become creative rather than adaptive,—the beauty of their imaginings coming from within, just as the beauty of nature is the efflux of the universal spirit" (163). Still, Stedman's is a functional idealism. He recognizes that concepts of beauty—and the appropriate means of expressing those concepts—do change with time and circumstance. Conservative as he basically was, Stedman certainly was not a reactionary, demanding that the artist utilize only traditional forms and styles.

Less flexible is Stedman's treatment, in the sixth chapter, of "truth" in poetry. As a committed meliorist, he insists on a positive, teleological approach to all experiences. Facts must be portrayed not so much in their own terms but for what they have the potential of revealing.

Realism, in the sense of naturalism, is the firm ground of all the arts, but the poet, then, is not a realist merely as concerns the things that are seen. He draws these as they are, but as they are or may be at their best. This lifts them out of the common, or, rather, it is thus we get at the "power and mystery of common things." His most audacious imaginings are within the felt possibilities of nature. But the use of poetry is to make us believe also in the impossible. (197)

Quite obviously, Stedman is not asserting a literary or Zolaistic naturalism, but a philosophical naturalism of the sort that rejects supernatural explanations. Nevertheless, he insists that each fact, every experience, if portrayed properly, should be capable of revealing both spiritual and material insight. We have seen that some of the "softer" realists also employed a teleological approach. For instance, Hamlin Garland offers a similar statement: "The realist or veritist is really an optimist, a dreamer. He sees life in terms of what it might be, as well as in terms of what it is; but he writes of what is, and, at his best, suggests what is to be, by contrast."[21] But it is hard to think of anyone pushing the doctrine to the point that Stedman does here. In the sense that this concept prevents the artist from dealing with things that are not "at their best," which means, in the last analysis, with the real world, it insulates him from the honest depiction of evil and pain. Further, it makes no provision for social criticism.

This extravagant meliorism is part of Stedman's attempt—continued and extended in the final two chapters, "Imagination" and "The Faculty Divine"—to resolve the problems of contemporary poetry. He blames its lack of passion and high imaginative power on a pervasive lack of faith. Each past age of great poetry had been based on some large and pervasive system of belief. Yet, such was Stedman's own faith in the power of poetry and such was his response to evolutionary theory and recent scientific discoveries, that he now suggests the grounds upon which a new faith could be based, one that will lead to the coming in the next century of a third great age of imaginative poetry to rival the Elizabethan and the Romantic. No longer the enemy, science is the source of a new inspiration.

In these final chapters, then, he offers the poet more than an aesthetic method, a specific subject matter, a celebration of the power of divinity in man. Evolutionary theory seemed to him to confirm the ancient biblical injunction, "Ye shall be as Gods." As had Bayard Taylor in *Prince Deukalion*, he suggests that the gap between man and God is narrowing. The God revealed by evolutionary theory, like man, creates "slowly and patiently, through ages and by evolution" (257). It is the poet, of course, who must play a central role in making manifest this new vision:

Now the artist not only has a right, but it is his duty, to indulge in an anthropomorphism of his own. In his conception the divine power must be the supreme poet, the matchless artist, not only the transcendency, but the immanence of all that is adorable in thought, feeling, and appearance. . . . As far as the poet, the artist, is creative, he becomes a sharer of the divine imagination and power, and even of the divine responsibility. (222–23)

Under the influence of high passion and guided by his divine imagination, the true poet, the genius, assumes the divine power of recreating the world, of finding the order and coherence that Stedman felt sure were at its center.

Stedman's "supreme poet" takes part in much the same tradition as Wallace Stevens' "supreme fiction." Indeed, Stedman, as a member of the Genteel Tradition, shares with both Stevens and Emerson a general approach to experience that Denis Donoghue has aptly summarized in discussing a passage from Emerson's *Journals*:

The only way to heal the breach between God, nature, and man is by becoming God and rearranging things according to your own "light." The occasion for doing so is provided (if we look ahead beyond Emerson to Wallace Stevens, the greatest poet in the genteel tradition) by the breakdown of supernatural belief and the confusions of epistomology. Hence we say, God and the human imagination are one. The saint is the man of thought. Emerson says (and the voice might well be Stevens') that "when the fact is seen under the light of an idea, the gaudy fable fades and shrivels." But he still speaks as a moralist. The answer to skepticism is the "moral sentiment, which never forfeits its supremacy."[22]

Stedman's purpose in *The Nature and Elements of Poetry* is nothing less than to "heal the break," to solve the twin problems of the continuation of poetry and of evil in the universe, by allowing the poet, in effect, to become God and rearrange the world according to the needs of his "divine" imagination. Stedman appropriates the universe to suit the needs of his ideal poet. It was precisely this "habit of mind" which, as one scholar has pointed out, Santayana "found everywhere in American letters. That habit of mind he called egotism or the anthropocentric conceit: the reduction of the universe to the categories of the mind that thinks it (idealism) and the enlisting of the cosmos on the side of some partial good (moral absolutism)."[23]

Stevens, however, was conscious of the fact that his myths were fictitious, invented to fill the vacuum created by the loss of religious tradition in the modern world. Emerson, as Perry Miller has shown, was so close to the Calvinist tradition of seeing nature as part of the divine fabric of the world that he was, in a sense, extending a native tradition.[24] But Stedman, working from his extreme interpretation of evolution, tries to exist in what we can recognize now as an artificial position between the two. His eagerness to promulgate such a poetics based on a melioristic interpretation of evolution reflects his own need at once to replace the lost faith of his youth and to make sense of the new world of science and technology. Ironically, he thought that he had based his poetics on the sure ground of scientific proof, on the latest theories from the physical sciences. And he felt that his investigation had been conducted with the systematic thoroughness of the scientist. In its pervasive optimism, *The Nature and Elements of Poetry* was true to one of the central assumptions of the age. From the perspective of this tragic century, however, we can see just how ill-founded and superficical this vision actually is.

CHAPTER 5

"What Need to Borrow?"
Stedman's Poetry

"HE cared most of all, in his heart of hearts, to be a poet, and saw that, while going afar to invoke the Muse, he had given her the less chance to seek him."[1] On several levels, Stedman's criticism of Taylor applies to his own creative life. It is doubtful, however, that he ever understood all the ways in which he went "afar."

He attempts to confront this problem in "Ariel," a poem addressed to Shelley and written during the centennial year of 1892. In two stanzas that correspond closely to stanzas five and six of Shelley's "Hymn to Intellectual Beauty," Stedman reviews the course of his poetic life:

> What joy it was to haunt some antique shade
> Lone as thine echo, and to wreak my youth
> Upon thy song,—to feel the throbs which made
> Thy bliss, thy ruth,—
> And thrill I knew not why, and dare to feel
> Myself an heir unknown
> To lands the poet treads alone
> Ere to his soul the gods their presence quite reveal!
>
> Even then, like thee, I vowed to dedicate
> My powers to beauty; ay, but thou didst keep
> The vow, whilst I knew not the afterweight
> That poets weep,
> The burthen under which one needs must bow,
> The rude years envying
> My voice the notes it fain would sing
> For men belike to hear, as still they hear thee now.[2]

There is pathos in the predicament of an older man, his artistic career virtually over, who, in yielding "once more" to the "heart of youth"

117

realizes the failure of his early hopes. Unable to keep the "vow," he has not created a living art. And since Shelley's poem is one of the first works of his poetic maturity, establishing the direction of his development, the contrast is the more striking.

But there is a broader pathos surrounding the entire performance. Stedman spoke proudly of "Ariel"; it was "poetry or nothing." Another time he called it "the most *poetical* poem I have written in many years."[3] Stedman uses the term "poetical" to mean "highly imaginative," but we are likely to apply it in certain of its negative connotations, "fanciful" or "factitious." In attempting at one and the same time to capture the inspiration of his childhood and the spirit of Shelley, he chooses a remote, highly "poetic" diction—"whilst," "antique shade," "didst," "afterweight," "burthen," "belike"—and this betrays him. Whereas Shelley describes a direct, ecstatic knowledge of "intellectual beauty," Stedman's inspiration, as in much of his poetry, is second-hand, primarily literary. For Shelley, intellectual beauty is an active force that leads man "to fear himself, and love all human kind." It is not a "burthen," but a spirit that brings with it a joy never "Unlinked with hope that thou wouldst free/ This world from its dark slavery." But Stedman's "vow" to beauty had not brought with it an active commitment either to search for self-knowledge or to fight for social justice. It lacks content. He had gone far, then, to seek the muse, not realizing, as had Whitman, that she might be found near at hand, in the life and language around him. He invented for "Ariel" a complex stanzaic structure, used here for the only time. But it leads to some awkward inversions and an expression that is not entirely clear.

Another tangible admission on Stedman's part of the failure of his career may be found in his decision to arrange his final collection topically rather than chronologically. As the "Publisher's Note" to the posthumous *The Poems of Edmund Clarence Stedman* explains, "shortly before his death Mr. Stedman gave directions for the preparation of a new volume, to contain all the poems which he deemed worthy of preservation, rearranged according to subjects, rather than, as is usual in collections of the kind, in the order of their original publication. The editors, in accordance with these instructions, have grouped the various poems, related either by subject or the occasion which produced them, in eleven sections." Stedman's decision was inevitable. One finds no consistent pattern of growth of development in his work. It remained a poetry in search of an appropriate subject or occasion.

Although Stedman sensed his ultimate failure as a poet, he was in fact remarkably successful in responding to public opportunities for verse. From the poems he subtitled "The Tribune Lyrics" of 1859 and 1860—"The Ballad of Lager Bier," "The Golden Wedding," and "How Old Brown Took Harper's Ferry"—to such late works as "Ariel," published in the *Atlantic* in 1892, and "Proem to an American Anthology," published in the *Century* in 1900, Stedman's poetry was constantly before the public. Although very little of this work survives, an analysis of it helps explain some of the social uses of poetry in America in the second half of the nineteenth century.

The largest of the eleven sections is "Poems of Occasion." Some of the works in this group, including the "Dartmouth Ode," "Hawthorne," "Corda Concordia," and "Mater Coronata," were read before audiences on various formal occasions. His public performances helped establish Stedman's contemporary reputation as one of the important poets of his generation, the poets born after 1820. Although most of the works in this group were not commissioned for delivery at some stated occasion, Stedman's inspiration, as in the case of "Ariel," was some significant public event, the death of a notable poet or soldier, or "the return to America of the remains of John Paul Jones," the subject of "Homeward Bound."

Much of the work in the other sections is also occasional. This is particularly true of the next two largest sections, "In War Time" (Civil War) and "Various Poems," which includes works on Helen Keller (a frequent subject for late nineteenth century poets in search of a theme), Oliver Wendell Holmes, foreign policy toward Cuba, and a visit to Chaucer's tomb. "The Carib Sea" section came directly from Stedman's two vacations to the region. "Poems of Manhattan" and "Poems of New England" are for the most part light verse in the local color vein. "Poems of Greece" consists largely of translations, from Homer, Theocritus, and Aeschylus. A long narrative poem set in the Middle Ages, "The Blameless Prince," which proved to be a poetic dead end, comprises another section. Finally, there is a short group of nature poems, a larger group of miscellaneous "Songs and Ballads," and a concluding section on death, "Shadow Land." In 1889 Whitman observed "a peculiar fact, that Stedman, though not very far from being an old man, seems to get more ardent the older he grows."[4] But one scarcely knows where to find the expression of this change among this grouping.

In his last letter to Taylor, Stedman confessed that while light emotions made him "easily loquacious," he was paralyzed when he came to feel deeply, a trait reflected in his poetry. When, as in "The Discoverer" or "Alice of Monmouth," he treats a potentially tragic theme, the point of the work seems to be to limit its threat, to circumscribe pain through sentiment. Whitman, in discussing the restraining or repressing principle in all of Stedman's work noted:

Stedman always feels that he must be judicial—the dominance of that principle has held him down from many a noble flight. Stedman seems so often just about to get off for a long voyage and stops himself on the shore. Why shouldn't we just let go—let life do its damndest: take every obstacle out of the way and let it go? Why should being thought foolish or unreasonable or coarse hold us back? We can go nowhere worthwhile if we submit to the scorners. [5]

Stedman fought to contain, not release, the emotions that continually threatened him, and his art became a means not of freeing and expressing his complex inner life, but of avoiding it.

The thematic groupings into which Stedman divided his poetry provide a convenient means of organizing and focusing a critical analysis of his work. However, since virtually all of these groups may be identified with particular periods of his life, it is also possible, through some rearrangement in the order in which the groups are considered, to approach Stedman's poetry both chronologically and thematically. Our subject, then, is his unsuccessful search for an appropriate metier.

II   "Poems of Manhattan"

Stedman's best poetry is regional, and is devoted not to his native New England but to his adopted Manhattan. The eight poems in this section may be classified as light verse. Preoccupied with the task of creating a lasting body of work, Stedman was unduly impressed with the obvious dangers of writing on the immediate and familiar. There are only eight works in this short section, and with the exception of "The Old Picture Dealer" (1883), all were written early in his career.

As we have seen in the example of "The Diamond Wedding," Stedman could employ light verse effectively for social satire. But with the exception of two inferior works that he did not retain, "The Prince's Ball" (1860), and "The House that Vander Built" (1869), he wrote only two other poems in this style: "Fuit Ilium" (1868), an attack on the senseless destruction of fine old New York homes to make way for ugly commercial structures, and "Israel Freyer's Bid for Gold" (1869), published in the *Daily Tribune* on September 28, 1869, which was a response to "Black Friday." Like "Watergate," the term "Black Friday" came to refer to a pervasive corruption in the nation's economic, political, and social system. It was on "Black Friday," September 24, 1869, that the infamous attempt of the Fisk-Gould syndicate to corner the country's gold market collapsed. The character "Israel Freyer" is based on Albert Speyers, whom Stedman described in his history, *The New York Stock Exchange* as an "elderly man of small intelligence," who was only a front or tool used by the syndicate.[6] Unfortunately, Stedman devotes so much attention to Speyres' frenetic and irrational trading on a day that brought financial ruin to many that his courageous attack on the real villain, Fisk, seems almost an afterthought:

> But it matters most, as it seems to me,
> That my countrymen, great and strong and free,
> So marvel at fellows who seem to win,
> That if even a Clown can only begin
> By stealing a railroad, and use its purse
> For cornering stocks and gold, or—worse—
> For buying a Judge and Legislature,
> And sinking still lower poor human nature,
> The gaping public, whatever befall,
> Will swallow him, tandem, harlots, and all!
> While our rich men drivel and stand amazed
> At the dust and pother his gang have raised. (95)

Stedman identifies the reciprocal relationship of an American public that worships success at any cost and the exploitive abuses of a "clown" like Fisk. If his social vision had been larger, he may well have been able to develop the art of exposing such abuses and cultural patterns; certainly there was ample material close at hand.

The remaining five poems of this section are written in a light style. Stedman creates a fanciful world somewhere between the recognizably real and the totally imaginary. As he remarked of "Peter Stuyvesant's New Year's Call": "I made a long and conscientious study for this ballad, trying, as in the "Ballad of Lager Bier" (1859), to ape the Flemish in their sense of the halo gilding real and common things."[7] The "halo" serves to heighten our appreciation of the real without falsifying it. In each of these works Stedman responds to the exciting, cosmopolitan quality of New York life by juxtaposing contemporary Manhattan with one or more of the earlier cultures that have become a part of it. For instance, in "Peter Stuyvesant's New Year's Call,"

which recounts a nostalgic, alcoholic visit of old Stuyvesant with a
crony, the reader comes to see that "Nieuw Amsterdam" is a loving
replication of the Holland of their memories. The Manhattan of 1860,
in turn, is a natural outgrowth of its predecessor of two hundred years
ago. In "The Ballad of Lager Bier," as Stedman and his close friend Tom
Harland, well-known around town as the manager of the Unitary
Home, come under the influence of a few drinks in Karl Schaeffer's
Manhattan Beer Hall, they find themselves visiting the evanescently
real Germany of their imaginations. For "Pan in Wall Street" (1867),
Stedman brings to life another well-known New Yorker, the man who
played "the real Pan's pipes around the Wall Street district," as he
reported to Howells. [8] "Bohemia" (1859) reflects the innocent excite-
ment both of the Bohemianism of the Pfaffian crowd and the earnestness of the Fourieristic communitarians. Among others, here is the
famous Queen of Bohemia, Ada Clare, "the bookish Sibyl,—she
whose tongue/The bees of Hybla must have fed." The miraculous
economic principles of the Unitary Home are described with affec-
tionate humor:

> And once we stopped a twelvemonth, where
> Five-score Bohemians began
> Their scheme to cheapen bed and fare,
> Upon a late-discovered plan;
> "For see," they said, "the sum how small
> By which one pilgrim's wants are met!
> And if a host together fall,
> What need of any cash at all?"
> Though how it worked I half forget,
> Yet still the same old dance and song
> We found,—the kindly, blithesome throng
> And joyance of Bohemia. (83)

The Civil War brought an end to the "joyance" of this Bohemia, and
Stedman's light art did not grow and develop in the postwar
environment that his "The Diamond Wedding" had prefigured. Yet
this group of Manhattan poems represents his most important
contribution to American poetry. As George F. Whicher has
remarked,

the typical contribution of [post–Civil War] New York poets was not made in
the vein of high seriousness. . . but in the minor genre of *verse de societé*, to

which the most readable work of Stedman, such as "Pan in Wall Street," may be said to belong. Written by a succession of clever journalists, editors, and college professors—beginning with George Arnold, William Winter, and other Bohemians of Pfaff's in the sixties, and extending down to the "Blue China" trifles of Henry Cuyler Bunner and Brander Matthews in the nineties—light verse proved itself the natural medium for the expression of the Manhattan mind.[9]

III *"In War Time"*

Like such contemporaries as George Boker and Bayard Taylor, Stedman enlisted his muse in the Union cause. Five of the eight poems in this section are short, highly charged editorial comments written for the New York newspapers. As a group they express the consistently aggressive attitude that Stedman held throughout the Civil War, from the time of John Brown's raid through the assassination of Lincoln. Each of these works exhibits Stedman's ability to create what has been called, in reference to Kipling, "a public emotion by swinging movement carefully varied in accordance with the demands of the particular theme."[10]

"How John Brown Took Harper's Ferry" appeared in the *Tribune* on November 12, 1859, midway between the attack (October 16) and Brown's execution (December 20). At the time, "Republican leaders, without exception, condemned the raid," in an attempt to quiet inflamed public opinion.[11] But in portraying Brown as a hero who has become slightly crazed in the service of a God-inspired cause, Stedman intends just the opposite, as this stanza shows:

Then he grasped his trusty rifle and boldly fought for freedom;
   Smote from border unto border the fierce, invading band;
And he and his brave boys vowed—so might Heaven help and speed 'em!—
   They would save those grand old prairies from the curse that blights the land;
         And Old Brown,
         Osawatomie Brown,
Said, "Boys, the Lord will aid us!" and He shoved his ramrod down. (3)

The ballad concludes by warning "Virginians" that if Brown is executed, they will find "A vengeful Fury, hissing through your slave-worn land!" (9). As Gay Wilson Allen has noted, the trochaic movement of the lines "reminds us of Hiawatha."[12] As with "Sumter," the purpose of this popular poem was to prepare the North for war. "Wanted—A Man" (1862) uses an insistent four stress rhythm and concludes each of the six octaves with the line, "Abraham Lincoln, Give us a MAN!" Each of these newspaper poems achieved a popular success. They do not, of course, survive as literature, but serve as excellent examples of the extensive use of verse for political or propagandistic purposes during our Civil War.

While Stedman's object in the newspaper poems is to intensify the immediate impact of a political event, the artistic effect of his long narrative poem, "Alice of Monmouth" (1863), is just the opposite. The suffering of war is bathed in such a warm, sentimental glow as to make it seem unreal. The fighting is portrayed in a manner reminiscent of the heroic, chivalrous battles of the Middle Ages. The political purpose of the work's melodramatic plot is to justify suffering as part of a divinely ordained struggle to purge the nation of sin and prepare the way for "a pure and holier union" (59). In this, the sentimental "Alice" apparently succeeded, as Lowell's emotional notice of the volume for the *North American* testified.[13]

But Stedman's interest in the poem may well have been as much with the opportunity the subject gave him to display his technical skills, to demonstrate that here was a young poet who has mastered his craft, as with the subject. The twenty stanzas of "Alice" employ a wide variety of metrical patterns, as Gay Wilson Allen has succinctly pointed out:

"Alice of Monmouth" contains practically every meter that was in use at the time, including octosyllable couplets, seven-stress quatrains, three-stress quatrains with initial trochees, the irregular ode arrangement, pentameter, heroic couplets, and two very unusual experiments, *viz.*: three-stress unrimed verse, with an iambic base . . . and unrimed alexandrines. . . . The alexandrines are reminiscent of Bryant's; some of the ode sections suggest comparisons with Whitman's war poems, such as "Beat! Beat! Drums!" and Stedman's whole verse technique is closely related to Lowell's versification.[14]

For his skill here and in the shorter newspaper verses, Allen asserts that "of all minor Civil War poets" Stedman's versification is most interesting for its range and variety."[15] But the war poetry exhibits a characteristic defect of so much of his verse, an accomplished technique unable to wrest the deeper meaning from its subjects, of artistry in excess of occasion.

IV   *"Poems of Greece"*

In *Harvests of Change*, Jay Martin observes, "immediately after the war, in a direct counteractant to the breakdown of consciousness and the loss of tradition that war always brings, [the established New England writers] turned almost as a group to the preservation of the landmarks of civilization, now in danger of being forgotten. They insisted upon the past by translating its classics."[16] As we have seen, Stedman began his translation of Theocritus shortly after the war, and was encouraged by Lowell.[17] While this translation provided the immediate occasion for Stedman's interest in the English hexameter, he sought to develop the hexameter to the point that it could take its place as a standard form for poetry in English. His fullest statement of this expectation comes in his review of Bryant's translation of Homer in the *Atlantic* for May 1872, where he predicts

that a resonant, swift metre will be developed, from elements now felt by our best poets to exist, which will have six accentual divisions, and hence may be called English hexameter verse; that it will partake of the quantitative nature of the intoned classical measures only through those natural dactyls not uncommon in our tongue, and through a resemblance which some of our trochees bear to the Greek spondaic feet; that it will be so much more the flexible, giving the poet liberty to shift his accents and now and then prefix redundant syllables; finally, that it often will have the billowy roll of the classical hexameter (as we moderns read the latter accentually).[18]

Stedman recognized the need for greater freedom—he sought the "billowy roll of the classical hexameter"—but his commitment to the accentual tradition was so strong that he could not work outside its confines. Taylor's success in reproducing the varied meters of Goethe's *Faust* in his translation (1870–71) stood as a commanding example of what could be done within the tradition.

Although Stedman invested a great deal of effort in his translation, the results, both in quality and quantity, are meager. In *The Blameless Prince and Other Poems* (1869), he published a portion of the Tenth Idyll, "The Reapers," and the Thirteenth, "Hylas," and retained these works in subsequent collections. But he did not add to this work. Over the years he attempted to establish an accurate text and worked on related scholarly problems. But surely his inability to perfect the sort of meter that could do all he had claimed for the English hexameter was responsible for this failure. In an 1880 letter, Parke Godwin forcefully told Stedman of his disappointment "that you should help keep alive. . .such a patent humbug as the English hexameter. Your short and hurried versions in the *Victorian Poets* [in "Tennyson and Theocritus"] are better. I agree fully with Landor, that all attempts at hexameter in English are abominable. In the first place, they are not hexameter, (dactyl and spondee), and when they are are utterly unmusical."[19] Perhaps if Stedman had not been so bound by the law "fidelity to form," he might well have been able to write a useful translation of Theocritus in free or iambic verse.

This section also includes two early treatments of classical themes, "Penelope" (1860) and "Alectryon" (1863). In the first, a direct response to Tennyson's "Ulysses," Penelope responds to her husband by insisting that she will not stay home alone, will not "linger in a widowed age," but instead will "cleave about/ Thy neck, with more than woman's prayers and tears,/ Until thou take me with thee" (242). In no sense can the poem stand the comparison with Tennyson that it so clearly invites. "Alectryon," which tells the story of the mortal who is turned into the cock by an "indignant" Ares, his erstwhile hunting companion, is far more interesting. Commanded to stand watch one night for the war god and the adulterous Aphrodite, Alectryon falls asleep, allowing Helios to discover the unwary lovers. Stedman initially considered the work his "*piece de résistance*" and was "chagrined" when Lowell ignored it in his *North American* review of *Alice of Monmouth*.[20] Several years later, when Stedman pressed him on the question, Lowell expressed a theoretical dislike for "these modern antiques. . . .They are all wrong. It's like writing Latin verses—the material you work in is dead. It's the difference between Chaucer and Gower." Rather reluctantly, Stedman came to agree: work in this form, in Lowell's phrase, could not be "an addition to poetic literature." Further, "a new land calls for new song."[21] He did not attempt any more "antiques."

Whatever one's theoretical objections to the genre might be, this particular work is enjoyable. And in dealing with the powerful attraction of the god of love and the god of war for each other, Stedman touches upon a basic human truth. His treatment of the theme, especially in poking fun at the pompous Ares, is appropriately and subtly humorous. The blank verse is flexible, and the use of sibilant consonants, while slightly obtrusive in places, helps establish a mood of languorous dalliance appropriate for the meeting of such magnificent lovers. While excitedly preparing for his night of lovemaking, Ares tells Alectryon:

> The Earth shall be at peace a summer's night;
> Men shall have calm, and the unconquered host
> Peopling the walls of Troas, and the tribes

Of Greece, shall sleep sweet sleep upon their arms;
For Aphroditê, queen of light and love,
Awaits me, blooming in the House of Fire,
Girt with the cestus, infinite in grace,
Dearer than battle and the joy of war:
She, for whose charms I would renounce the sword
Forever, even godhood, would she wreathe
My brows with myrtle, dwelling far from Heaven. (244)

Composed in Washington during the Civil War, "Alectryon" could well be placed in the "War Time" section. Through its gentle irony, it makes an important point: "make love, not war."

V *"The Blameless Prince"*

Of course it is impossible to speculate just what Stedman might have done with the antique if he had not been convinced by Lowell's argument rejecting this minor genre. But in denying himself this form, he complicated in a small way what he saw as his great problem, the search for an appropriate theme. In an 1873 letter to William Winter, Stedman observed: "You may be sure that whatever failure such men as you experience grows out of the *only* difficulty in our literary life—want of *themes* suited to *our* tastes and aspirations."[22] He had in mind particularly the inability to find appropriate subjects for long narrative poems. In addition to "Alice of Monmouth," he published only one other long poem, "The Blameless Prince" (1869), a narrative dealing with love, adultery, and death in a medieval kingdom. Since Lowell, in his first letter to Stedman, had praised *Alice* as "Christian, modern, American, and that's why I like her," Stedman felt that he must justify his choice of a remote setting to him:

What you say in your [Joseph] Quincy article in the *Atlantic*,[23] about the lack of contrast in American life is sharply true. Wishing to analyze certain passions and depict certain romantic conditions, I have been compelled to invent a medieval fable—much against my feeling as an American poet,—but are there any bounds to time and place in Art? One has, after all, to write what habitually comes to him. I have long had an American theme in mind, which will require strong and generous handling, but shall never touch it till I have riper poetic assurance than at present.[24]

The poem attacks the cult of Victoria and Albert by inverting the image of Albert's "unsullied purity." As Stedman explained to Taylor, "it struck me how *dramatic* it would be, if such a man as he, (say a medieval Prince), so married, etc., and bearing such a character in the sunlight of the world, had *really* a secret *liason*, lasting through all his life, with some woman he really loved, etc., etc.—"[25] The reader sympathizes with the prince in being yoked to the naively innocent, passionless queen. In the figure of the darkly gorgeous paramour, Stedman attacks the Victorian myth that women are not sensual beings. The poem exposes the hypocritical practice of many societies in holding up unrealistically austere standards of conduct. And while it does not condone adultery, the poem exposes the sham of the loveless marriage: "yet bonds of gold, linked hands, and chancel vows,/Even spousal beds, do not a marriage make" (276). As suggestive as the theme is, however, the poem's dramatic impact is blunted by the use of a medieval fable. While the subject may have been suggested to Stedman by certain realistic observations, these are lost to the reader in the transposition to the patently fictitious medieval kingdom. The characters never come fully alive; they are not the "individuals, men and women, various and real," which, in *Poets of America*, he would call upon the American poet to create. While the verse reads smoothly enough, the stanzaic structure, ababcc, leads the poet into some embarrassingly obvious rhymes:

> In that first glimpse each read the other's heart;
> But not without a summoning of himself
> To judgment did the Prince forever part
> From truth and fealty. As he pondered, still
> With stronger voice Love claimed a debt unpaid,
> And youth's hot pulses would not be gainsaid. (277)

It is simply impossible to take the prince's "hot pulses" seriously.

VI   *"Poems of Occasion"*

Unable to find the "riper poetic assurance" to execute his own themes, during the next decade Stedman accepted invitations to write and deliver long poems on such occasions as the 1873 commencement exercises at Dartmouth ("Beyond the Portals"), the unveiling of "The Monument of Horace Greely," the 1877 public meeting of the Harvard Phi Beta Kappa ("Hawthorne"), and the opening session of the Concord Summer School in Philosophy in 1881 ("Corda Concordia"). In these public poems, Stedman could not avoid the magniloquent and absolutely deadly rhetoric that the occasions invited. After all, the poet was forced to compete with the day's orator for the attention of the audience, and the accepted rules of the game allowed a certain compositional laxity. Of Lowell's "Commemoration Ode," widely accepted as the lofty realization of the genre, Stedman observes, "the weaker divisions of the production furnish a background" to the memorable passages.[26] None of Stedman's work in this genre survives as living poetry, and his own quotation from Lowell's "Centennial Ode" in *Poets of America* is apt:

> Poets, as their heads grow gray,
> Look from too far behind the eyes,
> Too long-experienced to be wise
> In guileless youth's diviner way;
> Life sings not now, but prophesies.[27]

Shortly after finishing the influential and widely acclaimed "Hawthorne," Stedman judged it his "highwater mark—as sustained, analytic, and imaginative, a piece, as I shall ever write."[28] Unlike "Beyond the Portals," which was modeled directly on the "Commemoration Ode," "Hawthorne" represents Stedman's own response to the challenge of the thirty minute public poem. He devised an elaborate stanzaic pattern. And the choice of a literary subject enabled him to marshall his critical faculties. As Edwin Cady has observed, the poem "took positions on most of the basic issues of the Hawthorne criticism of the time."[29]

The unique power of Hawthorne's work, Stedman suggests, is directly related to his ability to confront his region's difficult and ambiguous cultural heritage. In this, Hawthorne, "the one New Englander," is preeminent. Responding to lingering doubts concerning Hawthorne's artistic sanity, the poem demonstrates that the isolation of his long and difficult apprenticeship, in which he was "taught by repression," was an essential prelude to a courageous cultural struggle. He was, inevitably, a divided man: "Two natures in him strove/Like day with night, his sunshine and his gloom." The "gloom" was the product of a rigorous Calvinism, the "stern forefathers' creed descended/The weight of some inexorable Jove/ Prejudging from the cradle to the tomb." But the blackness of Hawthorne's work is balanced by a "light," "that Arcadian sweetness undismayed/Which finds in love its law" (188). The immediate inspiration for this compensating affirmation of the light was his experience of the New England landscape; ultimately it expresses Hawthorne's belief in divine grace. Stedman demonstrates the pervasiveness of these two elements, the light and the dark, in Hawthorne's work by continual and specific reference to situations and characters in the fiction.

But sympathetic as Stedman's approach to Hawthorne is, he will go only part way. He rejects with faintest praise the Hawthorne who questioned the Civil War and, more basically, "Progress":

> Was it not well that one—
> One, if not more—should meditate aloof,
>   Though not for nought the time's heroic quarrel,
> From what men rush to do and what is done.
> He little knew to join the web and woof
>   Whereof slow Progress weaves her rich apparel,
> But toward the Past half longing turned his head.
> His deft hand dallied with its common share
> Of human toil, nor sought new loads to lift
>   But held itself, instead,
> All consecrate to uses that make fair,
>   By right divine of his mysterious gift. (186)

While in one sense championing Hawthorne, the poem also seeks to defend the audience from him: no one need disturb his faith in the justness of our national goals or in "Progress." Nor need the contemporary artist, as had Hawthorne, "meditate aloof," opposing the direction of American culture. The essential moral and social battles have been won already.

Cady has shown just how pervasive the image of Hawthorne as a kind of artistic "wizard" was at this time. Stedman, however, will not be outdone in his elaboration of it:

> What sibyl to him bore
> The secret oracles that move and haunt?
>   At night's dread noon he scanned the enchanted glass,
> Ay, and himself the warlock's mantle wore,
> Nor to the thronging phantoms said Avaunt,
>   But waved his rod and bade them rise and pass; (186–87)

The rhetorical purpose of such characterizations, which serve almost to remove Hawthorne from the race of mortals, is to deflect the commanding power of his artistic vision, to put some distance between reader and artist. Stedman, who knew Hawthorne's work well and refers to it perceptively, might well have succeeded in this poem if he had been content to write simply and directly, to compose a tribute from a lesser artist to a master of infinitely greater courage and skill. There is something of this in "Hawthorne." But the rhetorical excesses that vitiate the poem may be traced to a pathetic attempt to bury Hawthorne in the very past that he had uncovered.

Yet this "defense" did define an image of Hawthorne which Stedman's contemporaries enthusiastically accepted. Holmes called the poem an "admirable contribution . . . at once to our poetical and critical literature," and Hawthorne's son Julian considered it "the most true and beautiful tribute yet made to Nath. Hawthorne's genius."[30] Cady has observed that with the publication of Lathrop's *Study* in 1876, this poem, and James's *Hawthorne* (1877), "Hawthorne became certified as an unchallengeable American genius." Stedman's poem is today the "least known" of these works, "But possibly, in its proper context [the] most significant."[31] Stedman's image of the novelist remained current throughout much of the remainder of the century.

Despite his public success as an occasional poet, to his credit Stedman grew increasingly restless in this role. After delivering "The Death of Bryant" before a memorial meeting of the Century Club in 1878, he decided to reject all further invitations for such poems. With but a few exceptions, e.g., "Corda Concordia" in 1881 and "Mater Coronata," delivered at the Yale Bicentennial in 1901, he adhered to this resolve, despite a constant stream of invitations.

But throughout his career Stedman continued to commemorate those picturesque and "poetic" occasions that regularly presented themselves. "On a Great Man Whose Mind Is Clouding," published in the *Atlantic* in March 1882, is a response to reports of Emerson's senility:

> That sovereign thought obscured? That vision clear
>   Dimmed in the shadow of the sable wing,
>   And fainter grown the fine interpreting
> Which as an oracle was ours to hear!
> Nay, but the Gods reclaim not from the seer
>   Their gift,—although he ceases here to sing,
>   And, like the antique sage, a covering
> Draws round his head, knowing what change is near. (207)

He celebrated the eightieth birthdays of Whittier ("Ad Vigilem," 1887) and Holmes ("Ergo Iris," 1889), and marked the passing of soldiers and poets. He always found a suitably elevated, dignified, and inspiring tone for these works; indeed, there is an unconvincing uniformity, a magniloquence, about many of them. Stedman was particularly concerned with celebrating the heroic wherever he could find it, and some of these works suggest that he found it in rather unlikely places, at least by contemporary standards. Particularly objectionable is "Custer" (1876), where the vainglorious general is praised as a "young lion of the plain," the "deathless spirit" of military heroism itself, while the Sioux Indians are characterized as a "wolfish foe," "red doomsmen" (172–73).

Mention should be made, however, of two gentle and successful elegies, "George Arnold" (1865), written shortly after the funeral of the young poet, and especially the moving "Horace Greeley," written in December 1872 for Stedman's former boss on the *Tribune*. The strain of his vigorous campaign for the presidency, his crushing defeat, and the death of his wife following in quick succession proved to be more than Greeley could stand. Stedman writes with pathos and sympathy of a great and humble man who could not find in others during his time of need the quiet kindness that he gave so freely:

> Alas that unto him who gave
>   So much, so little should be given!
> Himself alone he might not save
>   Of all for whom his hands had striven.
> Place, freedom, fame, his work bestowed:
>   Men took, and passed, and left him lonely;—
> What marvel if, beneath his load,
>   At times he craved—for justice only! (165–66)

"Horace Greeley," unlike many of the works in this section, is a concrete and specific portrait of its subject; it expresses the dignified and tender tone of the *Greek Anthology*, "so pathetic—and so human."[32]

VII *"Songs and Ballads"*

When W. D. Howells as editor of the *Atlantic* "invented the idea of having a song with music" in each number of the magazine, he inaugurated the feature by carrying Stedman's "Creole Lover's Song," with music by Dudley Buck, in the issue for January 1877: "I carried that feature through a year," he recalled, "but I saw it was not making any favor for the magazine, so I gave it up. No song was so successful as his."[33] In his essay on Procter for *Victorian Poets*, Stedman sadly noted a decline in contemporary song making, and in

1878 confessed to Richard Grant White to having " 'set up' for a song-writer; though this vulgar age and generation know and care little enough about song."[34] As the popularity of the "Creole Lover's Song," inspired by his trip to the Caribbean, indicates, Stedman did achieve a fair amount of contemporary success as a songwriter. At least nine different composers published settings for one or more of his songs. The popular "Song for a Drama" (1875) was set to music by at least five composers. However, he worked closely with only one, the American composer Dudley Buck, whose "To the Poet," opus 79 (1878), incorporates five of Stedman's poems: "Undiscovered Country," "Stanzas for Music," "Song for a Drama," "Creole Lover's Song," and "Nocturne." Stedman himself described these songs as "very fine in melody *and* harmony, with nothing commonplace in them."[35]

This comment, which may suggest something of the Victorian taste in song, points to what is, from a contemporary perspective, their glaring weakness, a lack of human immediacy and naturalness. This is especially true in the love songs, as the following stanza from "Nocturne" indicates:

> O life! O rarest hour!
>   When the dark world onward rolls,
> And the fiery planets drift,
>   Then from our commingled souls
> Clouds of passion and of power,
>   Flames of incense, lift! (380–81)

There is "nothing commonplace" about such language. The lover is not so much speaking with anyone in particular, least of all his beloved, as addressing an assembled audience. If Stedman had not felt such an unbridgeable gap between himself as artist and the "vulgar age," he might have written for a broader audience and given to his work the naturalness and immediacy that it so sorely lacks. In the process, he denied himself the full resources of the living language.

VIII *Vacation Poetry*

The fifteen poems of "The Carib Sea" section came directly from Stedman's two voyages to the region, in 1875 and 1892. Since the works in this section and in the "Poems of Nature" grouping betray their origins as vacation poems and since both sections are touched by an obtrusive moralism, it will be convenient to consider them together. The presence of moralism may seem ironic in view of Stedman's well-known opposition to didacticism, which in *Poets of America* he called a "trying habit . . . inbred as it seems, with the New England poets, most of whom have preached too much in verse."[36] The nine "Poems of Nature" betray their author's New England background. For instance, "Refuge in Nature" (1863) is, as the title implies, a kind of "brief" for the therapeutic values of the country to those lost in "the world's relentless war" (306). "The Freshet" (1860), although increasing as an attempt to capture in blank verse the direct, plain speech of the countryman, draws a familiar moral from the disaster it describes: "so true love conquers all" (305). The poet is so concerned with asserting some external truth that nature itself is not a strong presence. They are, quite obviously, the work of the tired and emotionally exhausted vacationer searching for emotional refreshment.

The fourteen Caribbean poems are arranged in a kind of sequence to represent the progress of a vacationer's trip to the region. He learns of the romantic legends of the region, of the pirates "Morgan" (1888) and "Captain Francisca" (1882), and is then entranced by the rich sensuousness of the tropics. In "La Source" (1897) he is haunted by the sight of naked native women bathing, particularly, a "defiant . . . wilding slip of womanhood" who

> stayed an instant, with one foot
> On tiptoe, poising statue-wise,
> And stared, and mocked us with her eyes,—
> While rippling to her hip's firm swell
> The mestee hair, that so outvies
> Europe's soft mesh, and holds right well
> The Afric sheen, in one dark torrent fell. (335)

But in the concluding work, "Martinique Idyll" (1882), we hear the voice of stern duty calling the idle traveler home to pick up the familiar burdens:

> Love is not perfect, sweet, that like a dream
>   Flows on without a forecast or a pain;
> Some burden must betide to make it strong,
> Some toil, to make its briefest bliss seem long,—
> Ay, longer than the crossing of a stream
>   Mist-haunted, lit by moons that surely wane. (356)

Once again we feel the ingrained Calvinism of Stedman's New England childhood compelling him to assume his "burden."

IX *"Poems of New England"*

Stedman recognized that he had been "injured for life and almost perished of repression and atrophy" in the Calvinistic back country of his childhood. But the closest he comes in his poetry to confronting the "stern forefathers' creed" is in "Hawthorne." Most of the eight "Poems of New England" deal with the picturesque and quaint qualities of the region. When Stedman does treat a tragic event, as in "The Lord's-Day Gale" (1873), which recounts the destruction of much of the Gloucester fishing fleet in a freak storm off the Canadian coast, we find the mawkish sentiment of emotional uplift and tearful acceptance:

> And wilt thou quail, and, dost thou fear?
> Ah no! though widows cheeks are pale,
> The lads shall say: "Another year,
> And we shall be of age to sail!"
> And the mothers' hearts shall fill with pride,
> Though tears drop fast for them who died
> When the fleet was wrecked in the Lord's-Day gale. (124)

Special attention, however, should be given to two modest but successful later works, "Cousin Lucrece" (1892) and "Huntington House" (1894). The first, a sketch in the manner of Holmes's "My Aunt," is based directly on a character whom Stedman remembers from his childhood. With sympathy and humor he tells of a ridiculous lady

> Living forlornly
> On nothing a year,
> How she took comfort
> Does not appear;
> How kept her body,
> On what they gave,
> Out of the poor-house,
> Out of the grave. (127–28)

In much the same style, "Huntington House" tells of the "Ladies Huntington. . .proud maidens four," for whom life is simply a preparation for entering the family burial ground, the oldest in town. These poems capture something of the mixture of pathos and humor that Stedman found in Holmes's best light verse.

X *"Various Poems"*

The thirty-eight works in this "grab-bag" section suggest the range of Stedman's search for an appropriate subject. "The Comedian's Last Night" (1875) is a dramatic monologue of a retiring performer, while in the sentimental "A Mother's Picture" (1860), Stedman speaks directly of his mother's hold on him: "This picture lingers; still she seems to me/ The fair young angel of my infancy" (400–401). This section contains the sternly patriotic, as in "The Hand of Lincoln" (1883), and meditative, regretful memories of forbidden love, "Estelle" (1873) and "Edged Tools" (1861). "Hebe" (1884) tells compactly of love, murder, and suicide among some circus performers; and in the philosophic "Fin de Siecle" (1892), Stedman affirms the hopeful promise of evolution for a dying and despairing century.

Perhaps the most interesting works in this group are the contrasting treatments of his "sense of failure in literature." In the early sonnet, "Hope Deferred" (1860), the artist, comparing his situation to that of a wild bird encaged in some alien region, is prematurely resigned: "Hopeless of all he dared to hope so long,/ The music born within him dies away" (400). But thirty-seven years later, in "Proem to 'Poems Now First Collected,' " he pathetically implores the "bright Spirit of song" to "renew, renew/ Thy gift to me fain clinging to thy robe!" Admitting a long "waste of years/ Filled with all cares that deaden and subdue," he pleads, "Still be thou kind, for still thou wast most dear" (454). In one of his last poems, "Music at Home" (1897), he at last opens his ears to the sometimes discordant music of a domestic muse. While in the country, reading a "deathless song" from ancient Greece, he is suddenly distracted by the intrusion of

> A catbird, riotous the world above,
> Hasting to spend his heritage ere love
> Should music change to madness in his throat,
> Leaving him naught but one discordant note.
> And as my home-bred chorister outvied
> The nightingale, old England's lark beside,
> I thought—What need to borrow? (434)

Stedman understood, however, that it was now too late for him to express in his song this new inspiration; the "Rhythm free and strong" of the catbird's "brave voice forecasts" the song of some future poet. "What need to borrow?" is a question he should have asked at the outset, not the conclusion of his career.

CHAPTER 6

The Library and Other Editorial Projects

O VER the course of little more than a decade, Stedman published four major editorial projects: *A Library of American Literature* (1888–90), with Ellen M. Hutchinson as "Junior Editor"; *The Works of Edgar Allan Poe* (1894–95), with George Woodbury; *A Victorian Anthology* (1895); and *An American Anthology, 1787–1899* (1900). Needless to say, he did not undertake these demanding editions as a way of filling up idle time. Heavily in dept as a result of his son's embezzlement in 1883, he was obliged to devote his working days to business. Each of these projects exacted a great deal of hard, detailed labor: obscure works had to be located and examined, selections chosen, copyright permission secured, authoritative tests established, volumes laid out, authors consulted, budgets met, secretaries supervised, and so on. But in each case, Stedman saw a job that had to be done, one which he simply could not refuse.

The most significant of the four editions is the *Library*. Through the eleven large volumes, comprised of selections drawn "from the earliest settlement to the present time," Stedman demonstrated conclusively something that was not generally accepted, that America possessed a literature of its own, a large and stimulating body of works written in a variety of genres that was both entertaining and reflective of the national experience. As the *Critic* expressed it in an early review: "Of course, the *raison d'être* of such a work is the belief in an American literature—in a sequence of writings which, produced under new conditions, increasingly embody a new spirit, and which are therefore worthy of separate and careful study."[1] We have to remember that at this time, as a result of a pervasive Anglophilia, American literature was virtually ignored. As Howard Mumford Jones has observed, "the inference that American topics, American genius, and American culture were inevitably barren was

138

extensively discussed."[2] Stedman exploded the myth of the poverty of American literature in the best possible way, by discovering and presenting representative samples that could speak for themselves and define their own tradition. Eschewing theoretical arguments and critical commentary, he presented American literature as an accomplished fact.

We have seen that in *Poets of America*, Stedman formulated an organic theory of American poetry, tracing a natural cycle of growth and decay. In the *Library*, he extends this approach to the national literature as a whole, demonstrating through his choice and arrangement of selections the existence of a body of literature that reflects the natural stages of growth of the nation. This demanded a broad conception of literature itself. Stedman included not only the expressly "literary," works written in the formal genres—poetry, fiction, and drama—but also such forms as travel chronicles, histories, sermons, political speeches and documents, letters, folk wisdom ("Popular Sayings"), ethnic literature ("Negro Hymns and Songs"), and folk songs. His clearest statement on this question is to be found in "The Growth of the American School," the second chapter of *Poets of America*. There, while taking a dim view of colonial poetry, he asserts that

the manifest, the sincere genius of the colonies is displayed elsewhere than in their laborious verse. Noble English and a simple, heroic wonder give zest to the writings of the early chroniclers, the annals of discovery and adventure. Such traits distinguish the narratives of the gallant and poetic Captain John Smith, and of Strachey, whose picture of a storm and wreck in the Bermudas so roused the spirit that conceived "The Tempest." They pervade the memorials of Bradford and Winthrop, of Johnson and Gookin, of Francis Higginson and Winslow and William Wood. There are power and imagination in the discourses of the great preachers,—Hooker, Cotton, Roger Williams, Oakes,—who founded a dominion of the pulpit that was not shaken until after the time of Edwards and Byles. . . . Law, religious fervor, superstition, were then the strength of life; and the time that produced Increase and Cotton Mather fostered a progeny quite as striking and characteristic as the melodists of our late Arcadian morn.[3]

This essay appeared first in *Scribner's* for October 1881, shortly before he began work on the *Library*.

Stedman saw that it would be fruitless even to discuss this subject when the literary documents themselves were available only in a few great libraries. The neglect of the texts had proceeded from the assumption that they were not worthwhile, and ignorance reinforced the assumption. The great accomplishment of the *Library* was to break this cycle by going "over the heads" of the professors of English literature and appealing directly to the people themselves, for whom the compilation was made. The reviewers, in such journals as the *Atlantic, Nation,* and the *Overland Monthly,* were surprised to find such vigorous and lively English in hitherto unsuspected sources.

The *Library* was the first work of its kind to appear since the Duyckincks' famous *Cyclopedia of American Literature* (1856), the predecessor work with which it is usually associated.[4] But it is important to note the differences. The *Cyclopedia* is primarily a reference tool. The subtitle reads "Personal and Critical Notices of Authors, and [in smaller type] Selections from Their Writings." Its purpose is to provide a comprehensive record of "what books have been produced, and by whom; whatever the books may have been or whoever the men." The exhibition of the writer's work is entirely secondary to the critical discussion, in the manner of our more elaborate textbook anthologies, of the writer's life and work. Stedman produced not a reference work but a series of intrinsically interesting writings. The only external apparatus included with the text is a bare statement of place and date of birth and death. The purpose of the *Library* is to allow each citizen the opportunity to come to know directly a representative selection of national literature, "with [his] own eyes."[5] Stedman expected that each of his readers would enjoy answering for himself the question that he quoted from Crevecoeur: "What is this American, this new man?"[6] Mark Twain's publishing firm, Charles L. Webster & Co., sold the *Library* through subscription.

Judging from the reviews, the two volumes devoted to *Early Colonial Literature, 1607–1764* and the volume on *Literature of the Revolutionary Period, 1765–1787* had the greatest impact. As the *Atlantic* pointed out, the selections were drawn from sources "rare or difficult of access, and many of them also are such that even a patient reader would never hunt out their contents."[7] In the preface, Stedman responds only briefly to the inevitable question as to why he is justified in terming works written by English subjects before the founding of the Republic "American:" the "spirit" of the early books and pamphlets "was one of independence and New World life. . . . We term all literature American that was produced by the heroic pioneers, whose thought, learning and resolution shaped the colonial mind."[8] And the reviewers agreed. As the *Atlantic* pointed out, "the fact that from the first [the Colonists] . . . looked on the land as their own and believed in it, and regarded their prosperity in a free condition as God's dealing with them was one fundamental ground underlying the entire revolutionary period. The Revolution was ingrained in them by their birth as citizens of the New World."[9] It was through the selections themselves, not some abstract argument, that the editors made their case for the national literature.

When he first began the project, Stedman later confessed, he did not "think the compilation of much import. It was merely a side-issue to me." But in the very process of compiling the *Library*, his opinion changed, and he felt that he and Miss Hutchinson had "*builded better than they knew.*"[10] As he wrote Walt Whitman, whose work was well represented, in sending the first seven volumes to him as a gift:

You will justly estimate its significance, and this quite irrespectively of its literary or artistic qualities. There are masterpieces in it. But it is *not* a collection of masterpieces: it is something of more moment to you and me. It is *America*. It is the symbolic, the essential, America from her infancy to the second Century of her grand Republic. It is the diary, the year-book, the Century-book, of her progress from Colonialism to Nationality. All her health and disease are here: her teething, measles, mumps, joy, delirium, nuptials, conflicts, dreams, delusions, her meanness and her nobility. We purposely make the work *inclusive*—trying to show every facet of this our huge, as yet half-cut, rose-diamond.[11]

The *Library* is the most radically *democratic* act that Stedman performed. As the *Atlantic* said of the first three volumes, the *Library* "is an illustration, better than any history," of the national life.[12] It is also eminently readable and enjoyable. In its broad conception of the nature of literature, in its discovery of neglected texts, and in its pattern of arrangement—in these and in other ways—the *Library* prepared the way for American literary scholarship as it is practiced today.

As the excerpts from the reviews in the *Atlantic* and *Critic* suggest, the major periodicals reviewed the work enthusiastically. Even the sober *Nation* urged its readers to purchase the series: "It would enrich any domestic library, and in all schools of the higher grade it should be on hand as an adjunct in teaching both history and literature, and as an aid in rhetorical exercise, whether reading, declamation, or composition."[13] Despite such notices, the *Library* was a commercial disaster, one of the great failures in American publishing history. It was more than a book; it was virtually a separate business unto itself. The expenses involved in editing, publishing, selling the work through subscription, and financing the installment payments were enormous. The original "projector" of the series, W. E. Dibble of Cincinnati, was forced to give up in 1886 after three years. The plates for five volumes had been stereotyped but no books had been published. The next year Stedman was able to save the project by convincing Charles L. Webster & Co. to purchase the *Library*. Under the agreement, the editors were to receive royalties of eight percent as well as a payment of $500.00 for each volume.

The Webster firm committed itself heavily to the project. Issuing the first three volumes in May 1888, it completed the series in the summer of 1890. During this time, as Twain reported to his friend Joe T. Goodman, the firm invested its entire annual operating profit from other operations, about $50,000 per year, as well as all receipts from sales, into the *Library*.[14] But even after publication had been completed, the *Library* continued to eat at the firm's capital. Since subscription sales of this multivolume edition were made on the installment plan, "Every sale . . . added to the [firm's] debt."[15] Unable to continue supporting the *Library* and unable to sell it as a separate business to another party, Charles L. Webster & Co. was forced into bankruptcy in 1894. The *Library* had, at last, brought down the entire house.

How could a work that had been reviewed so enthusiastically become such a financial disaster? Two factors stand out. For one thing, Stedman overestimated his audience in presenting to them large, "undigested" portions of the national literature. The average reader simply was not equipped to read critically; he wanted not the thing itself but interpretive studies of it. In the preface to the eleventh volume, the editors reported that "in response to many suggestions from the press and the public," for secondary reading materials, they had decided to include in this volume " 'Short Biographies' of all writers represented in the compilation" written expressly for the series by Arthur Stedman.[16] And more importantly, as became apparent to Fred J. Hall, who had taken charge of the ailing Webster firm in 1888, the days of subscription publishing were over. Hall wrote Twain in December 1890: "Outside of *L.A.L.*, I think the future of our business will depend quite largely upon the trade."[17] Even Twain's own *A Connecticut Yankee* (1889) had not done well as a subscription volume. Needless to say, the failure of the

Library, a project in which both men in different ways had invested so heavily, became a source of friction between them.[18]

After the unexpectedly great labor and aggravation of the *Library*, Stedman determined not to undertake additional editorial projects. But when the young Chicago publishing firm of Stone and Kimball approached him late in 1893 about doing a complete edition of Poe, it was impossible for him to refuse once the publishers accepted his stipulation that George Edward Woodberry be hired as co-editor.[19] After all, Poe's influence on Stedman had been enduring, as he confesses in his introduction to the "Tales": Poe "started a revolt against 'the didactic' and was our national propagandist of the now hackneyed formula, Art for Art's Sake, and of the creed that in perfect beauty consists the fullest truth. The question of his influence in this wise, upon later enthusiasts, would lead us forthwith into the by-ways of personal confession, of individual experience and result."[20] Stedman's production of the edition was itself a gesture of gratitude.

The Works of Edgar Allan Poe appeared in ten volumes, with illustrations by Albert Edward Sterner. Stedman contributed three lengthy essays, critical-historical introductions for the tales, poetry, and criticism. Woodberry wrote the "Biographical Memoir" and, as the "text expert," assumed chief responsibility for the text. In this regard, the major contribution of the edition was in establishing a reliable text for the poetry. On the other hand, the editors "reprinted the tales from Griswold's imperfect text;" it does not meet modern standards of textual scholarship. But its contemporary significance resulted primarily from the recognition given to Poe as a major American writer. As a poll taken by the *Critic* revealed, there were still widespread doubts in the 1890s that a writer thought to be degenerate in his personal habits could have a healthy influence.[21] Unfortunately, what Harriet Monroe called the "iciest New England formalism" of Woodberry's biography did little to counteract this position. But in his three essays Stedman manages to shift attention to Poe's artistic genius, arguing that the essential Poe is to be found in the literary work. Monroe concluded her review enthusiastically: "It is difficult to exaggerate the importance of this edition to our conception of Poe. For the first time his work has careful editing, all irregularities of text and eccentricities of punctuation being removed. And what is more important, Mr. Stedman gives the tales a symphonic unity by his orderly arrangement."[22]

While working on the Poe edition, Stedman was also preparing his

A Victorian Anthology, which he intended as a companion to *Victorian Poets.* The subtitle reads, *Selections Illustrating the Editor's Critical Review of British Poetry in the Reign of Victoria.* This enormous volume contains some 744 pages of double-columned text and includes 343 individual poets, fourteen from Australasia and twenty-two from Canada. Virtually every writer mentioned in *Victorian Poets* is represented, and Stedman did his best to include as well poets from the latest generation. Accordingly, the writers stretch from Landor to Yeats and A. E. (George Russell). There is a short biographical sketch of each writer. The inevitable price that this anthology pays for the range and breadth of coverage is thinness, especially in its representation of the major figures. For this reason, it falls short of its stated purpose, to illustrate the critical views of *Victorian Poets.* We have nothing here, for instance, of Tennyson's "In Memoriam" or of Swinburne's "Ave Atque Vale." Such "minor" poets as Arthur O'Shaughnessey, Robert Bridges, Austin Dobson, William Schwenk Gilbert, and many others properly belong in a collection such as this. But Stedman simply was not critical enough; he included too many poetasters. Perhaps he felt the need of competing with A. H. Miles's *Poets and Poetry of the Century,* which was then issuing from the press (1891–1897). Nevertheless, *A Victorian Anthology* did enjoy a remarkable commercial success. But if he had been more restrictive in passing out tickets of admission, he might well have better served the major and minor figures truly deserving a place at the anthological banquet table.

An American Anthology (1900) is an even larger compilation, including in its 773 pages of double-columned text over 550 poets. The "Biographical Notes" alone cover fifty-one pages and there is a twenty page introduction. In 1919 Lewis Untermeyer called it "a gargantuan collection of mediocrity and moralizing," and certainly from the modern perspective there is much—very much—that does not belong here.[23] But in putting together this anthology, Stedman was guided by a different set of principles than those followed by modern anthologists. It is instructive to contrast Stedman's practice with that of F. O. Matthiessen, who, in the preface to the *Oxford Book of American Verse* (1950), explicitly formulates the editorial principles that had guided him.[24] Matthiessen's rules correspond so directly to points made by Stedman in his preface that it is almost as if he were responding directly to him. There was complete agreement on only one rule—in Matthiessen's words, "not too many sonnets." Both recognized the potential danger of excerpting portions from longer works, but Stedman is not reluctant to break the rule. Seemingly reacting directly against Stedman's practice of including too many poets, Matthiessen established the rule of "fewer poets, with more space to each." His next two rules would also seem to be explicit rejections of Stedman's practice: include nothing that "the anthologist does not really like" and nothing on "merely historical grounds." Stedman comments that as much as he would have enjoyed creating an "eclectic" collection composed only of his favorite selections from the best American poets, that has not been his intention. He has instead sought to present an historical survey of "the choicest and most typical examples" of American poetry.

Stedman was guided, then, by two possibly contradictory standards, the quality of a work "as poetry," and "its quality as an expression and interpretation of the time itself."[25] Clearly more poets were able to pass through the second gate than the first. But one of Stedman's main purposes in editing the *Anthology* was to demonstrate that poetry, even if temporarily moribund, had once played a significant role in the national life:

Our own poetry excels [the English] as a recognizable voice in utterance of the emotions of a people. The storm and stress of youth have been upon us, and the nation has not lacked its lyric cry; meanwhile the typical sentiments of piety, domesticity, freedom, have made our less impassioned verse at least sincere. One who underrates the significance of our literature, prose or verse, as both the expression and the stimulant of national feeling, as of import in the past and to the future of America, and therefore of the world, is deficient in that critical insight which can judge even of its own day unwarped by personal taste or deference to public impression.[26]

Up until the dominance of prose fiction in the seventies, poetry was widely read—it was "the staple of current reading," "a 'force.'" Especially in the work of such figures as Longfellow, Bryant, Emerson, Lowell, and Whittier, American poetry "assumes its ancient and rightful place as the art originative of belief and deed."[27] While this is a rather extreme statement about a matter that is very difficult to measure precisely, Stedman is right in asserting that at one time poetry did "matter." And one purpose of the *Anthology* is to provide a full record of this cultural impact.

This is not to say that Stedman confuses literary or aesthetic excellence with cultural impact. Of the three greatest American poets, Poe, Whitman, and Emerson, only one, Emerson, may be said to have been a public "force." Nevertheless, there is a certain democratic appropriateness that these three writers were not members of a school, but found "inspiration from within, instead of copying the exquisite achievements of masters to whom we all resort for edification. . . . Our three most individual minstrels are now the most alive, resembling one another only in having each possessed the genius that originates. Years from now, it will be matter of fact that their influences were as lasting as those of any poets of this century."[28]

It is clear, however, that Stedman erred in including far too much work by second and third rate figures. Ironically, he felt that he had been far more restrictive than his predecessor in the field, R. W. Griswold, and quotes approvingly the statement of Dr. English that Griswold's "sins were not of omission but of commission."[29] Still, we have generous selections from the significant American poets of the century, including Lanier and Dickinson, and representation is given to anyone who might possibly merit inclusion. Finally, recognizing that the poets who had come of age during the nineties were already producing important work, Stedman devoted a large section, "Close of the Century," to such writers—many were personal friends—as Richard Hovey, Philip Henry Savage, Stephen Crane, George Cabot Lodge, William Vaughn Moody, and Edwin Arlington Robinson.

Probably the best review of the volume is Oscar L. Triggs' notice in the *Forum*. As did many reviewers, Triggs praises the editor's breadth: "Mr. Stedman holds all in the balance, and is capable of entertaining the shy transcendentalism of Jones Very, the passionate patriotism of Lowell, the free spirit of Garland, the heroic realism of Whitman, the sweet lyricism of women, and the sensuous, fawn-like graces of Hovey's 'Songs of Vagabondia.' Another compiler might make a different book—but I do not think it would be so representative, so fair, or so just a book as this 'Anthology'."[30] But Triggs goes on to raise a broader question, the question that, he feels, Whitman would raise: has American poetry, the poetry of the *Anthology*, actually been representative of American life? The question contains its own answer; he explicitly rejects Stedman's assertion that "our own poetry excels as a recognizable voice of utterance of the emotions of a people." On the contrary, American poetry had been written for the most part by men engaged in practical affairs, and their work is occasional. His final judgment of the *Anthology*, then, is Whitman's judgment on the great mass of American poetry itself: "American poetry is an expression of mere surface melody, within narrow limits, and yet, to give it its due, perfectly satisfying to the demands of the ear, of wondrous charm, of smooth and easy delivery, and the triumph of technical art. Above all things it is fractional and select. It shrugs free with aversion from the sturdy, the universal, and the democratic.' "[31]

CHAPTER 7

"Friend and Helper of Young Aspirants"

IN August 1889, Edwin Arlington Robinson, writing from Cambridge to his friend and fellow poet William Vaughn Moody, reported, "my conscience tells me that New York is the place for me. I must have the biggest conglomeration of humanity and inhumanity that America affords."[1] Paradoxically, it was in the comparative anonymity of New York that Robinson felt he could best immerse himself in American life. In moving to New York in October 1899, the unknown Robinson faced an uncertain future. But along with such contemporaries as Ridgely Torrence, Percy Mackaye, and Moody, he learned, as had earlier poets, that the friendship and assistance that Stedman was able to give helped make survival in the metropolis possible.

Stedman had met Robinson briefly several years earlier, and when he learned that the shy Robinson had returned to New York, he took the initiative in renewing their relationship. Stedman's granddaughter, Laura, wrote Mrs. Richards, a mutual friend of both poets, that after learning of Robinson's address, he "called very shortly, and as both the young celibates (as he calls them) were lonely and miserable they became good friends."[2] Indeed they did, and we can see something of the importance of this relationship for Robinson in the following excerpt from an August 1900 letter to Daniel Gregory Mason:

My chief recreation is riding to [Stedman's suburban home in] Bronxville on Sundays and consuming Mr. Stedman's tobacco. His doctor will now allow him to consume it himself, therefore my work in that line is a kind of profitable charity. Sometimes we go to the back lot behind his house, where we sit on ant hills and talk about farming and what is Art. He likes me because I wrote a thing called *The Clerks* and because I represent so many distinct varieties of imperturbable asininity. I am always pretty much the same, and I

148

fancy my influence is rather restful. The man is not at all well, but he keeps up a show of cheerfulness and really likes to have all sorts of damned things come to see him. He has a world of good stories to tell of New York forty years ago and he quotes one golden saying by R. H. Stoddard which all of us should paste in our hats. "The public," says R.H.S., "will never know how much of your stuff you strike out."[3]

The major differences in age, social standing, and literary reputation would seem to preclude a close friendship between the two writers. But Stedman had a special concern for the many younger poets and critics who sought his advice and friendship, and there can be little doubt that he enjoyed these visits quite as much as Robinson did. He was able to help him in other, more tangible ways as well, most notably by publishing five of his best poems in *An American Anthology*.[4]

Stedman did more than simply offer younger poets genial hospitality and friendship: he read and criticized their work, helped them find publishers, "loaned" money, wrote letters of recommendation, reserved a large section of the *Anthology* for a generous selection from their work—he did whatever he could to further their careers, to make life possible for them as poets. And in this way, he made an important contribution to our literary life, one which, as Gregory and Zaturenska have noted, lived on after him: Stedman "had the gift of extending nicely tempered encouragement to poets who had not quite arrived, and his conduct probably (since she was often among his younger guests) offered an example to Harriet Monroe. Certainly the heritage of courteous and yet inspiring hospitality (that made a visit to *Poetry's* office in Chicago an event in the lives of many younger poets) and remained unbroken."[5]

I *"A Word Even from Me"*

The assumption of the role of fatherly adviser and encourager became an exceptionally healthy way for Stedman to transform his own feelings of insecurity, his life-long need for just such support. Even in 1890, at fifty-seven, he was instantaneously reduced to tears upon learning that Whittier had dedicated *At Sundown* (1890) to

E.C.S.

Poet and friend of poets, if thy glass
Detects no flower in winter's tuft of grass,
Let this slight token of the debt I owe
Outlive for the December's frozen day,

> And, like the Arbutus budding under snow,
>   Take bloom and fragrance from some morn of May
> When he who gives it shall have gone the way
> Where faith shall see and reverent trust shall know.[6]

Whittier's phrasing of this inscription indicates that he recognized Stedman's unusual need for reassurance and support.

That Stedman was aware of the interrelationship between his childhood insecurity, his search for a surrogate father, and his assumption of that role is made clear in his letter of thanks to "My Dear—My Beloved—Mr. Whittier":

> On this afternoon of the day when my mother *would* have been 80 years old, I came home fatigued and sad, not knowing that you had provided for me the keenest pleasure I now have experienced for many a day—and certainly the highest honor that has come to me at any time. When Laura, my wife, handed me the copy of "Sundown," I saw tears in her eyes and a smile on her face. I am not ashamed to confess that before I had finished reading the exquisite inscription to E.C.S., and what with weakness and surprise and gratitude and a rush of tender feelings, I was myself crying like a child.
>
> Indeed, I have grown old without having time to realize it or to outgrow the selfsame thoughts with respect to you and your work that I had when a youth in New England. *You have put your hands upon my head and blessed me.* No other hands, no other blessing, can be so dear to me—though other blessings come where one like yours has fallen.
>
> No poet older than myself, except Bayard Taylor, has ever understood me as you have—or said to me such words as you have said from time to time. Perhaps my own lack of such warmth *from above* has made me a little more thoughtful to those still younger who care for a word even from me.[7]

Paradoxically, then, Stedman was able to give to younger poets much the same kind of emotional support and reassurance for which he looked to Whittier. But in changing roles and in giving instead of receiving, he found a particularly effective way of controlling—if not overcoming—the insecurity which continued to threaten him throughout his life.

II *The New York Connection*

As we have seen, as far back as the late 1860s, Stedman had predicted the emergence of New York as the country's literary center. The growth in the New York publishing business in succeeding decades was phenomenal. But as Stedman complained in

Poets of America, this "somewhat uncongenial city" had no tradition of integrating literary men into the broader social fabric.[8] There was no central magazine or university, as Boston had the *Atlantic* and Harvard, around which to build a literary life. The responsibility for nurturing such a life, Stedman saw, would have to be accepted by individuals. As a newcomer to the city, he had enjoyed the gatherings at the home of the Stoddards, and he welcomed the opportunity in later decades to do his share. Since both he and Laura liked entertaining together, it was almost inevitable that their home would become a central meeting place. American poets, established and unknown, both New Yorkers and visitors, sought him out, as did many writers visiting from abroad. He had extensive friendships in the New York publishing, newspaper, and artistic communities, and enjoyed forgetting about business in the company of non-businessmen. As it became financially possible, the Stedmans regularly opened their home. Harriet Monroe recalled, "the Stedmans' famous Sunday evenings . . . brought together everybody who was anybody in the arts, whether native or foreign, residing in the metropolis or arriving from afar."[9]

A careful host, Stedman avoided taking too active a role in the conversation. He was much more concerned, as Hamlin Garland reported, with tempting "his guests to talk and often went so far as to have one or two 'address the meeting' on some ethical or esthetic subject. Good music was often heard in these rooms."[10] Harriet Monroe's report is similar. Stedman and Laura

knew how to keep their parties going, so that sympathetic guests met each other and antipathetic ones were kept apart. Visiting actors . . . would take the place by storm for an hour or two; and literary highlights were always shining there. The urbane Richard Watson Gilder, the self-protective William Dean Howells, the important Robert Underwood Johnson, the much overrated Edith Thomas, the lively Frances Hodgson Burnett, the dynamic Joseph Pulitzer—these and many other famous or aspiring writers and editors would occasionally enliven these evenings.[11]

These regular Sunday evenings and other more or less formal entertainments provided younger writers with a natural means of getting to know—and be known in—the New York literary world. But it is well to remember Monroe's observation that the man who so blithely presided over these affairs, "the acknowledged leader of New York's literary group," was "at heart never satisfied, in spite of his picturesque superficial vanity, with what the muse had granted him, and longing in vain to retire from Wall Street and write the immortal poem."[12]

A visiting or newly arrived writer did not have to wait for a formal invitation from Stedman. His door was always open—to the unknown and established alike. For Hamlin Garland, who visited with him frequently during the 1890s, Stedman was one of the "saving graces of New York":

Sprightly, airy, not too refined, a boy with the boys, he refused to grow old. . . . He knew almost every distinguished writer in England and America, by correspondence at least, and his judgments, on the whole, were sound. There was nothing malicious or bitter in his criticism. Like Gilder and Howells he desired to be helpful and was especially hospitable to young poets. Perhaps, like Howells, he sometimes took promise for achievement, but our verse writers needed just such an advocate at this time.[13]

Stedman, in describing the "twilight of the poets" in *Poets of America*, had also predicted a poetic renaissance. He welcomed the opportunity to validate this predication by helping, in whatever way he could, the younger poets who might possibly fulfill it. In this regard, a letter from Ridgely Torrence shows just how strenuous Stedman's "advocacy" could be:

There has been delay in the sending of my book [*El Dorado*] to you because I wanted first to write in it. As I send it, I think of all its history, of the time I appeared at "Casa Laura" [Stedman's Bronxville home] with it and found you on a sick bed. I think of how you read it as best you could during that illness and then I remember that Sunday a few weeks later when you were just able to sit up and to be about a little and you walked with me through the blazing sun of late June to Mr. Moody's and did what you could to find me a publisher. Do you think I shall ever forget it? Everything good, everything worth while, all the real things that have come to me since I went to New York, seven years ago, have come through you. Through you I have met all the friends I have since known. The longer I live the more I realize what you have done for me.[14]

Here was one area in which Stedman was able to overcome the "genteel split" of his life; through such service, he was able to bring together his literary ideals and actions in the physical world.

III *National Critic*

Stedman's reputation as the leading critic and advocate of

American poetry was national in scope, and he regularly received in the mails, unsolicited, from all over the country, books and manuscripts for his review and comment. So heavy did the resulting burden of correspondence become that in 1879 he was forced to prepare a form letter explaining that he could no longer:

(1) Read any Mss. sent me, nor give advice concerning them;
(2) Offer any person's Mss. to an editor or publisher;
(3) Engage to deliver poems or addresses, upon ordinary occasions, before societies, etc.;
(4) *Respond to miscellaneous requests for service, and to literary and other communications not essential to my regular work.* [15]

While he managed in this way to avoid writing verses for "ordinary occasions," he could not hold to his first two resolves. Indeed, he seems to have used this letter more as a convenient way of avoiding having to say something unpleasant about work that he did not like than as an excuse to avoid reading, and commenting on, that which showed genuine promise.

This was the case with Lizette Reese, who sent Stedman a copy of her first volume, *A Branch of May* (1887). He responded with "a very kind and sympathetic letter"[16] which, as her own letter in response shows, meant a great deal to the Baltimore poet.[17]

> 1407 N. Central Ave.
> Baltimore, Md.
> March 5, 1888

Mr. Edmund C. Stedman:
A little while before Christmas I mailed you my book of poems,ˣ and received in return a letter so brimful of encouragement and kind wishes that I must heartily thank you for it.
If I ever succeed in making something of myself—as you seem to think I can—I will always count your letter as one of the principal means to that end.
> Respectfully
> Lizette Woodworth Reese

ˣ*A Branch of May*

Reese reports in her autobiography, *A Victorian Village*, that this letter "started a long and firm friendship."[18]
Stedman helped advance her career in other ways as well. He brought her poetry to the attention of William Sharp ("Fiona Macleod"), the English poet and romanticist, who included "Tell Me

Some Way" in his anthology, *American Sonnets* (1889).[19] (Incidentally, Sharp, who was Stedman's house guest in the fall of 1889, dedicated this volume to him, as "The Foremost American Critic.") A letter of April 3, 1891, from Reese to Stedman shows that Stedman was responsible for bringing *A Handful of Lavender* to the attention of Houghton, Mifflin, which published the volume the next year.[20] But for Reese, it was the man himself, not what he might be able to do for her, that mattered. She often stayed with the Stedmans during trips to New York,

first at his New York house in Fifty-seventh Street, and afterwards at the one on a hillside in Bronxville. . . . Everybody of consequence as artist, novelist, poet came back and forth to these unlocked, cheerful doors, raw young writers like myself, seasoned writers, and old, eager friends ready to renew past companionships. It was like one of those gay and friendly London mansions in the flashing eighteenth century.[21]

Just how important these visits became for her is suggested in her letter to Stedman of April 7, 1899. I quote the concluding paragraphs:

We are so dull here in Baltimore. We know so little about Art, and we *think* we know so much. Still, it is a great deal for me to feel I have stood by my guns. Yes, it pays.

Dear Poet, I really believe I am going to write some more verse. Something I thought I had lost has come back again.

It began to blossom at your house, (the heavenly time I had there quickened it), and now it has blown out, and I am the happiest creature in the world. I tell you, because you understand.

This is the last letter of all. I have kept my best wine for the end. Dear, dear Poet, I send you my love, and you are not to answer this.

Affectionately,
Lizette Reese

Stedman included a generous selection of her work in *An American Anthology*, and his brief characterization there shows that he recognized the distinctive qualities of her art: "Miss Reese's poetry is of a rare quality,—artistic, natural, beautiful with the old-time atmosphere and associations, and at times rising to a noble classicism."[23] One of the best brief evaluations of her work appears in Gregory and Zaturenska's *History of American Poetry, 1900–1940*. After crediting Stedman with being one of the poet's "first admirers," they quote from his introduction to *An American Anthology* in which he asserts that even in this "twilight interval" there "continues an exercise of the art by many whose trick of song persists under all conditions."[24] Gregory and Zaturenska conclude:

It is extremely doubtful if any interval, however twilight, could have kept Lizette Reese from writing the poetry she chose to write for, as it has been said before, she was one of those rare writers whose seemingly effortless grace and freshness sustained the illusion of her being a "born poet" and her undidactic lyricism gathered its rewards throughout the three decades, when in the full tide of poetic upheaval and experimentation, all sides paused to do her honor.[25]

My purpose in discussing the Reese-Stedman friendship in such detail has not been to imply that all of his relationships with younger poets followed this model. These relationships—and the help he was able to give—were as different as the individuals involved. He encouraged Emma Lazarus to write on the Jewish subjects that meant so much to her and urged Laura Richards not to neglect her poetry for children. He discussed blank verse with Edwin Markham and helped Richard Hovey find a publisher. In these and many other ways, Stedman's active concern made a difference.

IV Terminus

During the last decade of his life Stedman enjoyed a particularly rewarding relationship with the youngest generation of American poets, which included Robinson, Moody, Torrence, Percy MacKaye, Richard Hovey, Josephine Peabody, and others. Coming of age in the 1890s, most of these writers came to New York, and at one time or another they were centrally concerned with writing poetic dramas for stage production. Quite naturally, then, they looked for guidance and inspiration to Stedman, who, as early as *Victorian Poets*, had called upon younger poets to work in dramatic forms. MacKaye has described Stedman as a kind of "Nestor" to this group:

Very different in spirit from that "money down"–presumption [of New York] was the creatively critical spirit of Edmund Clarence Stedman, who was then the acknowledged Nestor of our native poetry in the New York metropolis. To his home in Bronxville, N.Y., poets and authors from England and America made pilgrimage. There, in 1900, Moody had dispatched the first advance copy of his first published book, *The Masque of Judgment*, writing him (Oct. 30), "Doubtless you are overwhelmed by tributes of this questionable kind, yet I am bold enough to hope you will read the book, even if it remains in your mind as a symbol of grotesquely ambitious 'first volumes'."[26]

Of course Stedman read this and other works of these poets, proudly went to the openings of their plays, and studied their work closely.

In a letter to MacKaye written in the spring of 1907, less than a year before his death, Stedman spoke approvingly of the direction, potential, and initial achievements of this group. He was not, however, fully satisfied. The bulk of the letter contains a diplomatically worded criticism in the form of sensible advice. He urged them to go beyond classical and other imitative subject matter and directly treat their own times. "You will not have done your work at all until you show some evidence in it of the spirit of a New World. . . . you only show your own limitations when you profess to show yourselves unable to find American atmosphere and themes for American dramas."[27]

Beneath the ostensible security and prosperity of his life at this time, Stedman experienced an uncertainty about his future not terribly different from that of these younger writers. With his retirement from business in 1900, he once again became dependent on his pen. As he analyzed the situation in his diary in January:

> Sold my "seat" in the New York Stock Exchange for $39,500. . . . This ends a membership of thirty and one-half years . . . and is like tearing a tree up by the roots. . . . It is the first chance, in seventeen years, for retiring with honor, though half the money goes to liquidate my debts to my dear comrade Baker who has carried me through evil times. And I am at best leaving the *raft* which has given me support since my ship was scuttled in 1883. Here at sixty-six, I don't know whether I have the strength to live by writing, and I have no other means of support. It *is* a jump into the big sea—and to swim or sink.[28]

Of course, the "scuttling" to which Stedman refers was his son's embezzlement of his firm's capital. Now he had to use half the proceeds from the sale of his seat to repay the loans he had taken out to stay in business. Although not poor, he had neither the wealth nor the leisure for which he was envied. In a diary entry the next month, he observed the public reaction to his retirement: "They all speak of my 'fortune'. I would it existed. They think I am to have perfect leisure to write fine works—whereas, I am frightened at the prospect.—What do we know of one another, anyhow? . . . . It seems to me a big Stedman myth."[29] His friendships with the younger writers provided one way to escape this entire situation. In going with Robinson to the back lot behind his house to talk of farming and art, he could forget about the "Stedman myth" entirely.

The years after his retirement until his death in January 1908 brought a full measure of aggravation, disappointment, and pain. In 1901, he agreed to edit and write large portions of a history, *The New York Stock Exchange* (1905). But "his last years were tormented that the Company [Stock Exchange Historical Co.]. . .failed to issue the second volume. . . . His strength and daily interest were given to the supervision of this work, and there are many records of value in existence proving how bitterly and unjustly he was tried by conditions over which he could have no authority."[30] During this time death took many of those closest to him: Elizabeth Stoddard in 1902, her husband the next year, and Aldrich in 1907. His older son, Fred, died in 1906, shortly after father and son had become reconciled after an estrangement of twenty-three years. This was only a year after Laura's death in 1905. Troubled by financial insecurity, he was forced to sell the Bronxville home. Although his health was comparatively good, he had been left a very much weaker man by the serious heart attack he suffered in 1899. He was able to write little verse, and only occasional criticism. He left his last major project, a volume of *Reminiscences*, uncompleted at his death. And, of course, he lived with the knowledge that he had failed in the major goal of his life, to create a lasting poetry.

But the man who endured these disappointments was not broken—indeed, he never became "an old man" at all. On the day he died, he was completing an essay, "The Prince of the Power of the Air," speculating on the implications for Britain's preeminent world position of the development of aerial navigation. The essay, published posthumously in the *Century*, reviews developments in aeronautics in the thirty years since Stedman had published a paper in the *Scribner's* for February 1879 predicting the coming era of flight and theorizing on the size, shape, and speed of air craft.[31] Certainly his interest in the work of younger poets did not abate. At the opening of MacKaye's *Sappho and Phaon*, which he attended with the author and his wife, Moody, Robinson, George Grey Barnard, and Howells, he "nudged his young poet friends and spoke glowingly again of his 'long-ago prediction of the dramatic renaissance of poetry.' "[32] His zest, that irrepressible boyish energy, had not left him. And neither had his willingness to follow through on his enthusiasms. MacKaye wrote:

On January 15, 1908, I spent a long evening with Stedman at his New York apartment where we talked of Moody, and our dramatic group, and of our future plans, and he recounted to me his own projected plan for a critical volume interpreting the first decade of the twentieth century in its tendencies of the new American poetry. The next day he died suddenly. Had he lived six months longer, Amy Lowell's volume. . .would have been nine years preceded by an authoritative critical survey from Stedman's pen. [33]

The sudden, massive heart attack that claimed Stedman the next afternoon took a man who survived the "repression and atrophy" of his childhood and endured long enough to achieve a unique victory.

CHAPTER 8

Summary and Conclusions

ALTHOUGH Stedman recognized early in the 1870's that the dominant tradition of Victorian poetry had been played out, he was not himself able to create in the newly dramatic style for which he called. He continued to employ the imitative style that he had formed on the model of the Romantics and Tennyson. The extraordinary reverence in which he and his closest associates held the established New England poets compounded the problem. As he admitted in *Poets of America*, by the time that he realized that these aged "veterans" were "running in grooves" it was too late for him to strike out on his own. And as he came to recognize had been the case with Bayard Taylor, Stedman's career choices interferred with the development of whatever creative talent he possessed. The conclusion is inescapable that as a poet Stedman was a willing victim of a singularly difficult period and if this were his only claim, his life and career would not warrant a full-scale study.

Yet, to pose the question in this way is also to suggest the basis of Stedman's success. He saw the limitations of his own verse, and from the early 1870s devoted his major literary energies to criticism and scholarly projects. This work was not entirely disinterested. He sought to understand the broad cultural forces that affected the writing of poetry, and in such essays as "Bayard Taylor" and "The Outlook" he took the measure of his own failure and that of his closest associates. Criticism served him as a means on confronting and overcoming the debilitating pressures of the Genteel Tradition.

More than a mere synthesis of the environmentalist perspective of Taine and the transcendentalist tradition, the critical strategy that he formulated was particularly well equipped to deal with the problems of contemporary literature. He demonstrated that the critic must see the work within its context, while recognizing that a work of art can

159

never be reduced to context. The critic's first obligation is to the work as an autonomous whole. Stedman spoke honestly and directly of his reactions to the poetry of such "dangerous" writers as Swinburne and Rossetti, Poe and Whitman. That his conclusions differed from the accepted moral canons made no difference: the critic's true business is with literary, not moral or philosophical, values. We can apply Brander Matthews' comment on the Whitman article to Stedman's criticism at its best; his is "criticism, cold, clean and true."

Stedman fashioned a prose style of definite strengths and limitations. Even at its best, his prose does not command attention for its own sake. And the modern reader may be put off by the sort of rhetorical elaboration that he comes across occasionally, as in the opening sentence of *Poets of America:* "It is my design to trace the current of poesy, deepening and widening in common with our streams of riches, knowledge, and power; to show an influence upon the national sentiment no less potent, if less obvious, than that derived from the historic records of our past; to watch the first dawning upon an eager people of'the happy, heavenly vision men call Art'; to observe closely and to set down with an honest hand our foremost illustrations of the Rise of Poetry in America". One objects to the archaic "poesy" and to the controlling metaphor. Poetry, we would like to answer, can not be put on the same level as "riches, knowledge, and power," and it should not be likened to a widening stream. To open the book with such an elaborate and balanced periodic sentence concluding with a phrase that is capitalized to give it even additional emphasis is an obviously contrived device. One also notices an excessive use of underlining for emphasis in Stedman's correspondence, evident even in his early letters. These devices may reflect a basic insecurity, a fear that when he makes his most important statements, the mere saying of the thing will not be enough.

However, the rigorous demands of the essay form as Stedman employed it forced him for the most part to avoid such rhetorical flourishes. The essays that make up his important volumes are not informal explorations of this or that theme. He sought instead to deal comprehensively and systematically with the major contemporary poets and to do so within the compass of a magazine article. The success of the Whitman article for such a reader as Henry Mills Alden was due precisely to Stedman's ability to consider all sides of the poet's genius. This of course required, as Stedman explained to O'Connor, that he write a "condensed paper." "If you know how I have resisted the temptation to be epigrammatic, & the number of my 'bright things' which I have cut out you probably would take those I have retained with a good unction."[1] Stedman recognized that good prose is not poetic and tested his work by the requirement that each sentence state a new fact or idea. Viewed within the essay as a whole, Stedman's prose is disciplined, structured, direct, and functional. In this way he made a major contribution to what Howard Mumford Jones has called "the true work of the genteel tradition," the disciplining of American prose, "a discipline of craftsmanship in the context of Western culture."[2]

In measuring Stedman's achievement, we can hardly ignore the narrow range and limited volume of his criticism. He wrote only two major volumes of practical criticism and a single theoretical work. Although his writing is informed by a grasp of the western poetic tradition from the Greeks onward, his central concerns were limited to nineteenth century poetry in English and the development of American literature. Within these bounds, however, he did make a number of impressive contributions, contributions for which he deserves a permanant place as an important American critic. *Victorian Poets*, which formulates an original critical method, also breaks new ground in its analysis of the effects of science on the imagination and convincingly relates this to the crisis of poetic style. This very popular volume, in addition to combatting the didactic, also helped prepare the way for the acceptance of realism in America by demonstrating the usefulness of the perspective of Taine, the "philosopher of realistic movement."[3]

The significance of Stedman's most important essays, on Poe and Whitman, has been recognized today. But what has not been seen is that in making room for Poe and Whitman as major poets within the American canon, *Poets of America* deflates the reputations of virtually all the others. Stedman avoided the simplistic rhetoric of attack and defense by relating each major writer to the larger theory of American poetry that he had defined. Anticipating the judgments of some of our best scholars and critics, his essays on such figures as Longfellow, Holmes, Whittier, and Taylor can be read not only for their historical value but also as criticism that is worth attending to. And since we are at a time when, as one scholar recently observed, "critics have compiled a sufficiently rich and detailed commentary on individual American poets to begin the tricky task of tracing the contours of a tradition (and of a countertradition as well)," Stedman provides the example of one who in his own time faced this "tricky task" head on.[4]

One value of his theory is that, while recognizing the central importance of Emerson, Poe, and Whitman, he was also able to define the lesser, but still significant, roles of the others he dealt with (excluding Taylor), particularly Bryant and Longfellow. Of course, not knowing Edward Taylor, he slights colonial poetry, and Emily Dickinson's verse became available too late for him to deal with it adequately. American poetry in the almost one hundred years since he wrote has been so rich and varied as to suggest complexities and achievements that he could not have imagined. But Stedman makes a strong argument that the major poets with whom he deals can be seen to form a single tradition that is related to the overall development of the national life.

Stedman's very concern with this problem suggests another dimension of his achievement. As the editors of *The Literary History of the United States* observe in their Preface: "each generation should produce at least one literary history of the United States, for each generation must define the past in its own terms."[5] Stedman accepted this challenge both in *Poets of America* and in his major editorial projects, most particularly the *Library*. The *Library* may be said to have begun the task of defining the past in this way for it demonstrated that America did indeed possess a national literature. As the vigorous letter which Stedman sent to Whitman in March of 1889 accompanying the gift of seven volumes makes clear, this was a project conceived in the spirit of Whitman's broad nationalism and executed with that poet's breadth and inclusiveness. Whitman was his ideal reader: "*You* of all men will take in, comprehend, the purpose, the meaning, of this long compilation."[6]

That he conceived of this important project with something of Whitman's broad vision of the national literature in mind suggests how far Stedman had come from the views of the "Defenders of Ideality" with whom he is usually associated. As a poet he did share in certain of their limitations , and his critical theory is vitiated, finally, by a failure to account for tragedy. But as critic, scholar, and man of letters he made a singularly original contribution to our literature. In his ability to focus his criticism on the literary work itself, he anticipated the new critics. In his prolonged war against the heresy of the didactic, he continued and extended the work of Poe. And perhaps most important, in his anthologies and critical works he gave new meaning to the concept of American literature. On another level, in his service to younger artists, he helped prepare the way for his long-predicted rebirth of poetry in America—something he did not live long enough to see.

Notes and References

Preface

1. Harriet, Monroe, *A Poet's Life* (New York, 1938), p. 82.
2. Jay B. Hubbell, *Who Are the Major American Writers?* (Durham, 1972), p. 99.
3. *A Library of American Literature* (New York, 1889), I, v.
4. Laura Stedman and George Gould, M.D., *Life and Letters of Edmund Clarence Stedman* (New York, 1910), II, 148–49.
5. *Victorian Poets* (Boston, 1875), p. 1.
6. George Santayana, "The Genteel Tradition in American Philosophy," in *Winds of Doctrine* (New York, 1913), p. 204.
7. Willard Thorpe, "Defenders of Ideality," in *Literary History of the United States*, ed. Robert E. Spiller et al., 3rd ed. rev. (New York, 1963), p. 809.

Chapter One

1. Letter, Edmund C. Stedman to Thomas W. Higginson, December 1, 1875. This letter is in the Houghton Library and is quoted by permission of the Harvard College Library.
2. Margaret Fuller, *A New England Childhood* (Boston, 1916), pp. 4–5.
3. Edwin D. Mead, "Introduction," David Low Dodge, *War Inconsistent with the Religion of Jesus Christ* (Boston, 1905), p. vii.
4. Stedman and Gould, I, 6. All future references to this work in this chapter will be cited in the text. This has been my major source for Stedman's life. I have also used unpublished letters from the Stedman Collection at Columbia and Margaret Fuller's biography of Stedman's early years, *A New England Childhood*.
5. William Rideing, *Many Celebrities* (Garden City, N.Y., 1912), p. 171.
6. *The Collected Writings of Thomas DeQuincy*, ed. David Masson (Edinburgh, 1890), XIII, 363–64.
7. On May 5, 1840, for instance, he wrote her: "I shall ask Grandfather if I can come and see you. I guess he will say yes, when I tell him you are sick don't you? and then I will try to comfort you and hope you will get well . . ." (I, p. 27).
8. Rideing, p. 170.
9. Fuller, p. 242.
10. Rideing, p. 171.
11. Ibid., 170.

12. Fuller, p. 242.

13. Rideing, p. 171.

14. Ibid.

15. Ibid., 170

16. C[harles] R. E[rdman], Jr., *DAB*, X, 418.

17. A. R. Macdonough, "Edmund Clarence Stedman," *Scribner's Monthly*, 7 (November 18, 1873), 58.

18. "Amavi," *Putnam's Monthly*, 4 (October 1854), 361.

19. *The Poems of Edmund Clarence Stedman*, (Boston, 1908), pp. 99–100 (hereinafter cited as *Complete Poems*).

20. Madeleine B. Stern, *Imprints on History* (Bloomington, 1956), pp. 193–94.

21. William Dean Howells, *Literary Friends and Acquaintance*, eds. David F. Hiatt and Edwin H. Cady (Bloomington, 1968), p. 75.

22. *Harper's New Monthly*, 21 (June, 1860), 118.

23. *An American Anthology, 1787–1899* (Boston, 1900), p. 823.

24. Mrs. Thomas Bailey Aldrich, *Crowding Memories* (Boston, 1920), p. 14.

25. Howells, p. 78.

26. *Poets of America* (Boston, 1885), p. 418.

27. Letter, Stedman to Taylor, November 18, 1878, in Richard Cary, "The Genteel Tradition in America, 1850-1875" (Ph.D. dissertation, Cornell University, 1952), pp. 219–20.

28. *Complete Poems*, pp. 9–10.

29. Louis M. Starr, *Bohemian Brigade* (New York, 1954), p. 357.

30. Ibid., p. 94.

31. Roy Meredith, *Mr. Lincoln's Contemporaries* (New York, 1951), p. 191.

32. Letter, Stedman to Taylor, January 25, 1863, in Cary, p. 188.

33. "Robes of Honor," *The Round Table*, 1 (December 26, 1863), 24.

34. *The Collected Writings of Walt Whitman: The Correspondence*, ed. Edwin Haviland Miller (New York, 1961), I, 167.

35. *North American Review*, 98, (January 1864), 293.

36. *Complete Poems*, p. 90.

37. *The Unpublished Letters of Bayard Taylor*, ed. John Richie Schultz (San Marino, 1937), p. 94. Letter dated October 31, 1866.

38. Cary, p. 193.

39. *Victorian Poets*, p. xvii.

40. Taken from three letters from Lowell to Stedman in 1866. See Stedman and Gould, I, 371, 375, 408.

41. Howard Mumford Jones, *The Age of Energy* (New York, 1971), p. 487.

42. Letter, Stedman to Taylor, May 21, 1866, in Cary, p. 193.

43. Letter, Stedman to Taylor, December 21, 1868, in Ibid, p. 200.

44. Frank Luther Mott, *A History of American Magazines: 1850–1865* (Cambridge, Mass., 1938), II, p. 419.

45. "The House that Vander Bilt," *Independent*, 21 (November 18, 1869), 3.

46. George E. Saintsbury, *A History of Nineteenth Century Literature* (New York, 1910), p. 259.

Chapter Two

1. Letter, Howells to Stedman. This letter is owned by Columbia University and is published with the permission of the university.

2. *Victorian Poets*, p. 1. All references to this work in this chapter will be given in the text.

3. "Victorian Poetry," *Scribner's*, 5 (January, 1873), 358.

4. Howard Mumford Jones, "Introduction" to William Cary Brownell, *American Prose Masters*, (Cambridge, Mass., 1967), p. x.

5. "Literature at Home," *Putnam's Magazine*, 8 (February, 1869), 242.

6. R. H. Stoddard, "Matthew Arnold," *Appleton's Journal*, 3 (January 8, 1870), 48.

7. *Poets of America*, pp. 336–37.

8. *Appleton's Journal*, 1 (April 3, 1869), 23.

9. Harry Hayden Clark, "The Influence of Science on American Literary Criticism, 1860–1910," *Wisconsin Academy of Sciences, Arts and Letters*, 34 (1955), 109–10.

10. *The Nation*, 14 (January 4, 1872), 10–11.

11. Jerome Buckley, "General Materials," in Frederick E. Faverty, ed., *The Victorian Poets: A Guide to Research* (Cambridge, Mass., 1968), pp. 15–16.

12. Robert Falk, "The Rise of Realism," in *Transitions in American Literature*, ed. Harry H. Clark (Durham, N.C., 1954), p. 440.

13. Edward Dowden, *Studies in Literature* (London, 1892), p. 85.

14. See Stanley T. Williams, "The Story of *Gebir*," *PMLA*, 36 (December, 1921), 630–31.

15. George E. DeMille, *Literary Criticism in America* (1931; rpt. New York, 1967), p. 143.

16. Comments taken from *ABC of Reading* (New York, 1960), pp. 185–87; and *Literary Essays of Ezra Pound* (Norfolk, 1954), p. 286.

17. John O. Eidsen, "The Reception of Tennyson's Plays in America," *Philological Quarterly*, 34 (October 1956), 436.

18. Henry James, "Mr. Tennyson's Drama," *Galaxy*, 20 (September 1875), 396.

19. Marshall McLuhan, "Tennyson and the Romantic Epic," *Critical Essays on Tennyson's Poetry*, ed. John Killham (London, 1960), pp. 88–89.

20. Ibid., p. 88.

21. Ibid., p. 82.

22. Clyde de L. Ryals, "Tennyson: the Poet as Critic: Appraisals of Tennyson by His Contemporaries," *Tennessee Studies in Literature*, 7 (1962), 123.

23. Saintsbury, p. 274.

24. Horace Scudder, "Recent Literature," *Atlantic Monthly* 37 (January 1876), 113.

25. See especially Robert O. Preyer, "Two Styles in the Verse of Robert Browning," *ELH*, 32 (1965), 62–84; and William Cadbury, "Lyric and Antilyric Forms: A Method for Judging Browning," *University of Toronto Quarterly*, 34 (October 1964), 49–67.

26. Stedman and Gould, I, 516; II, 44.

27. Letter, Ezra Pound to W. C. Williams, October 21, 1908. *The Letters of Ezra Pound*, ed. D.D. Paige (New York, 1950), pp. 3–4.

28. Philip Drew, *Robert Browning: A Collection of Critical Essays* (London, 1966), p. 6.

29. Stedman and Gould, II, 65.

30. Anonymous, "Prose Essays by Poets," *North American*, 123 (July 1876), 216–21.

31. Clyde Kenneth Hyder, *Swinburne's Literary Career and Fame* (Durham, N.C., 1933), p. 24.

32. Stedman and Gould, I, 375.

33. *The North American Review*, 103 (July 1866), 239.

34. Stedman and Gould, I, 408.

35. *The Swinburne Letters*, ed. Cecil Lang (New Haven, 1960), III, pp. 8–16.

36. Stedman and Gould, II, 153.

37. Letter, Dr. Holland to Stedman, December 27, 1874. This letter is owned by Columbia University and is published by permission of the University.

38. Ibid.

39. Letter, Swinburne to Stedman, February 20, 1875, in Lang, III, 8.

40. William Fredeman, *Pre-Raphaelitism, A Biblio-critical Study* (Cambridge, Mass., 1965), p. 235.

41. Stedman and Gould, II, 39.

42. See C. Cornelius Weygandt, *The Time of Tennyson* (New York, 1936), pp. 233–34.

43. Richard Henry Stoddard, *The Late English Poets* (New York, 1865), p. vi.

44. Robert Buchanan, "The Fleshly School of Poetry," *The Contemporary Review*, 18 (October, 1871), 334–50.

45. Ibid., p. 350.

46. *Harper's*, 40 (April 1870), 775.

47. *Atlantic*, 30 (June 1870), 752.

48. DeMille, pp. 144–45.

49. John Chubbe, *Victorian Forerunner* (Durham, N. C., 1968).

50. *The Poetical Works of Matthew Arnold,* eds. C. B. Tinker and H. F. Lowry (London, 1950), p. xviii.

51. Walter Houghton, *The Victorian Frame of Mind* (New Haven, 1957), p. 302.

52. *The Nature and Elements of Poetry*, (Boston, 1892), pp. 134–35.

53. R. H. Stoddard, *Appleton's Journal*, 4 (September 17, 1870), 351.

54. Stedman and Gould, I, 475.

55. DeMille, p. 145.

56. Virginia Woolf, "Aurora Leigh," *Yale Review*, 20 (Summer 1931), 677–90.

57. Stedman and Gould, I, 526.

58. Edmund W. Gosse, *Transatlantic Dialogue*, eds. Paul F. Mattheisen and Michael Millgate (Austin, 1965), p. 61.

59. Stedman and Gould, II, 59.

60. Paul F. Mattheisen and Michael Millgate, "Introduction," *Transatlantic Dialogue*, p. 6.

61. Quoted in Frank Luther Mott, *A History of American Magazines*, II, p. 399.

62. Malcolm Cowley, "American Books Abroad," in *Literary History of the United States: History*, p. 1376.

Chapter Three

1. Stedman and Gould, I, 487–88.

2. Ibid., I, 501–502.

3. Ibid., I, 529.

4. Ibid., I, 551.

5. *The New York Stock Exchange* (1905; rpt. New York, 1969), pp. 285–86.

6. Cary, p. 220.

7. Quoted in Benjamin T. Spencer, *The Quest for Nationality* (Syracuse, 1957), p. 295.

8. Holland, "Our Garnered Names," *Scribner's*, 16 (October 1878), 896.

9. Ibid., p. 895.

10. Spencer, p. 295.

11. Ibid., p. 301.

12. Richard Grant White, "Americanism in Letters," *New York Times*, (February 1, 1880), 7.

13. *Poets of America*, p. 7. All future references to this book in this chapter will be cited in the text.

14. Cary, p. 220.

15. Donald Ringe, "Kindred Spirits: Bryant and Cole," *American Quarterly*, 6 (Fall 1954), 233–44.

16. Donald Hall, "Whittier," *The Texas Quarterly*, 3 (Autumn 1960), 165.

17. Robert Penn Warren, *John Greenleaf Whittier's Poetry* (Minneapolis, 1971).

18. Hall, pp. 173–74.

19. Lewis E. Weeks, Jr., "Whittier Criticism Over the Years," *Essex Institute Historical Collections*, 100 (July 1964), 168.

20. William Torrey Harris, "Ralph Waldo Emerson," *The Atlantic Monthly*, 50, (August 1882), 244, 246.

21. Van Wyck Brooks, *America's Coming of Age* (New York, 1924), p. 50.

22. Quoted in Richard Croom Beatty, *Bayard Taylor* (Norman, 1936), p. 345.

23. *The Nation*, 30 (April 29, 1880), 327.

24. Dudley R. Hutchinson, "Poe's Reputation in England and America, 1850–1909," *American Literature*, 14 (November 1943), 216.

25. George Parsons Lathrop, "Poe, Irving, Hawthorne," *Scribner's*, 11 (April 1876), 802–803.

26. Werner Hofmann, *The Earthly Paradise* (New York, 1961), p. 241.

27. Quoted in Spencer, p. 295.

28. Jay B. Hubbell, "Poe" in *Eight American Authors*, ed. Floyd Stovall (New York, 1956), p. 21.

29. *The Nation*, 40 (January 29, 1885), 98.

30. Barry Menikoff, "Holmes," in *Fifteen American Authors Before 1900*, eds. Robert A. Rees and Earl N. Harbert (Madison, 1971), p. 214.

31. W. H. Auden, "Introduction," *The Oxford Book of Light Verse* (New York, 1938), p. ix.

32. Menikoff, p. 214.

33. Ibid., p. 222.

34. Letter, Stoddard to Taylor, December 8, 1868, in Cary, p. 154.

35. Ibid., 198.

36. Letter, Stedman to Lowell, May 31, 1882. This letter is in the Houghton Library and is quoted by permission of the Harvard College Library.

37. Charles B. Willard, *Whitman's American Fame* (Providence, 1950), pp. 23–24.

38. Included in my "Whitman and the Magazines: Some Documentary Evidence," *American Literature*, 44 (May 1972), 245.

39. Letter, Brander Mathews to Stedman, October 18, 1880. This letter is owned by Columbia University and published with permission of the University.

40. Letter, Dr. Maurice Bucke to Stedman, June 12, 1880. This letter is owned by Columbia University and is published with permission of the University.

41. Scholnick.

42. "Walt Whitman," *Scribner's* 21 (November 1880), 52.

43. Letter, William Sloane Kennedy to Stedman, December 1880. This letter is owned by Columbia University and is published with the permission of the University.

44. John Burroughs, "Walt Whitman and His 'Drum Taps,'" *Galaxy*, 2 (December 1, 1866), 147–48.

45. Josephine Miles, "The Poetry of Praise," in *Whitman: A Collection of*

Critical Essays, ed. Roy Harvey Pearce (Englewood Cliffs, N.J., 1962), p. 174.

46. Letter, Henry Mills Alden to Stedman, November 16, 1880. This letter is owned by Columbia University and is published with permission of the University.

47. Stedman and Gould, I, 375–76.

48. *The Nation*, 29 (November 27, 1879), 366.

49. Edwin Arlington Robinson, *Collected Poems* (New York, 1937), p. 93.

Chapter Four

1. *Poets of America*, p. xiv.

2. W. D. Howells, "Editor's Study," *Harper's Magazine*, 72 (March 1886), 647.

3. Ibid.

4. Quoted in *Representative Selections*, eds. Clara and Rudolf Kirk (New York, 1950), p. cxxxvi.

5. Howells, p. 648.

6. Jane Johnson, "Introduction," in Hamlin Garland, *Crumbling Idols* (Cambridge, Mass., 1960), p. xviii.

7. Howells, p. 650.

8. Kirk and Kirk, p. cl.

9. Howells, "The Editor's Study," p. 649.

10. Johnson, p. xvi.

11. Kirk and Kirk, p. cxliv.

12. Reprinted in *Genius and Other Essays* (New York, 1911), p. 16.

13. Ibid., pp. 20–21.

14. Ibid., p. 24.

15. Ibid., p. 35.

16. Stedman and Gould, II, 148.

17. Ibid., p. 150.

18. *The Nature and Elements of Poetry*, p. viii. All future references to this work in this chapter will be cited in the text.

19. DeMille, p. 152.

20. Jones, *The Age of Energy*, p. 484, n. 9.

21. Garland, p. 43.

22. Denis Donoghue, *Connoisseurs of Chaos* (New York, 1965), pp. 15–16.

23. Richard Cotton Lyon, "Introduction," *Santayana on America* (New York, 1968), p. xxi.

24. Perry Miller, "From Edwards to Emerson," *The New England Quarterly*, 12 (1940), 589–617.

Chapter Five

1. *Poets of America*, p. 415.

2. *Complete Poems*, pp. 201–204. All future reference to Stedman's poetry in this chapter are to this edition and are given in the text.

3. Stedman and Gould, II, 419.

4. Horace Traubel, *With Walt Whitman in Camden*, V (Carbondale, 1964), p. 328.

5. Ibid., I (New York, 1915), p. 78.

6. *History of the New York Stock Exchange*, p. 223.

7. Stedman and Gould, I, 220.

8. Ibid., p. 400.

9. George F. Whicher, "Poetry After the Civil War," in *American Writers on American Literature*, ed. John Macy, (New York, 1931), pp. 378–79.

10. *Norton Anthology of English Literature*, II (New York, 1962), p. 1266.

11. Wilfred E. Binkley, *American Political Parties* (New York, 1962), p. 228.

12. Gay Wilson Allen, *American Prosody* (New York, 1935), p. 151.

13. James Russell Lowell, Untitled Review, *North American Review*, XCVIII (January 1864), 293.

14. Allen, p. 151.

15. Ibid., p. 150.

16. Jay Martin, *Harvests of Change* (Englewood Cliffs, N. J., 1967), p. 12.

17. Stedman and Gould, I, 409.

18. "Recent Literature," *Atlantic Monthly*, 29 (May 1872), 623–24.

19. Letter, January 20, 1880. From typescript, Columbia University Library. This is owned by Columbia University and is quoted with the permission of the university.

20. Stedman and Gould, I, 372.

21. Ibid.

22. Ibid., pp. 466–67.

23. James Russell Lowell, "A Great Public Character," *Atlantic Monthly*, 20 (November 1867), 618–32.

24. Letter, December 2, 1867. This letter is in the Houghton Library and is quoted by permission of the Harvard College Library.

25. Stedman and Gould, I, 419.

26. *Poets of America*, p. 344.

27. Ibid., 345.

28. Stedman and Gould, II, 286.

29. Edwin Cady, " 'The Wizard Hand': Hawthorne, 1864–1900," in Roy Harvey Pearce, ed. *Hawthorne Centenary Essays* (Columbus, Ohio, 1964), p. 323.

30. Stedman and Gould, II, 287; 297.

31. Cady, p. 321.

32. *The Nature and Elements of Poetry*, p. 88.

33. Stedman and Gould, I, 536–37.

34. Ibid., p. 539.

35. Ibid., p. 540.

36. *Poets of America*, p. 215.

Chapter Six

1. "The Stedman-Hutchinson Library," *The Critic*, 13 (July 28, 1888), 38.

2. Howard Mumford Jones, *The Theory of American Literature* (Ithaca, 1948), p. 121.

3. *Poets of America*, p. 34.

4. Evert Augustus Duyckinck, *Cyclopaedia of American Literature* (New York, 1856).

5. *A Library of American Literature* (New York, 1889), I, v.

6. Ibid., III, 142.

7. "A Library of American Literature," *Atlantic Monthly*, 62 (September 1888), 423.

8. *Library*, I, vii.

9. "A Library of American Literature," 423.

10. Stedman and Gould, II, 127.

11. Ibid., p. 121.

12. "A Library of American Literature," 420.

13. "A Library of American Literature," *Nation*, 46 (June 14, 1888), 495.

14. *Mark Twain's Letters*, ed. Albert Bigelow Paine (New York, 1917), II, 546.

15. *Mark Twain's Letters to His Publishers*, ed. Hamlin Hill (Berkley, 1967), p. 299.

16. *Library*, XI, vi.

17. In *Mark Twain's Letters to His Publishers*, 262–63.

18. See especially Twain's letter to Fred J. Hall, December 22, 1891, in *Mark Twain's Letters to His Publishers*, 296–98.

19. Woodberry, a poet who was teaching at Columbia, had published a biography of Poe in 1885.

20. *The Works of Edgar Allan Poe* (Chicago, 1894), I, 120.

21. Cited in Hubbell, *Who Are the Major American Writers?*, p. 53.

22. Harriet Monroe, "Chicago Letter," *Critic*, XXVI (January 5, 1895), 15–16.

23. As quoted in Hubbell, *Who Are the Major American Writers?*, p. 100.

24. F. O. Matthiessen, "Introduction," *Oxford Book of American Verse* (New York, 1950), pp. ix–xiii.

25. *An American Anthology*, p. xxii.

26. Ibid.

27. Ibid., pp. xxii–xxiii.

28. Ibid., p. xxiv.

29. Ibid., p. xvii.

30. Oscar L. Triggs, "A Century of American Poetry," *Forum*, 30 (January 1901), 631.

31. Ibid., 640.

Chapter Seven

1. Letter, E. A. Robinson to W. V. Moody, August 1899. "Robinson to Moody: Ten Unpublished Letters," ed. Edwin Fussell, *American Literature*, 23, (May 1951), 174.

2. Letter of July 11, 1900, in Stedman's letter book for January-October 1900, Columbia University. For a complete discussion of the Stedmans' relationship with Mrs. Richards and Robinson, see my essay "The Shadowed Years; Mrs. Richards, Mr. Stedman, and Robinson," in *Colby Library Quarterly*, 9 (June 1972), 510–31.

3. Daniel Gregory Mason, "Some Early Letters of Edwin Arlington Robinson," *Virginia Quarterly Review*, 13 (Winter 1937), 67–68.

4. Stedman included "Luke Havergal," "Ballade of Dead Friends," "The Clerks," "The Pity of the Leaves," and "The House on the Hill." *An American Anthology*, pp. 727–29.

5. Horace Gregory and Marya Zaturenska, *A History of American Poetry: 1900–1940* (New York, 1946), p. 12.

6. John Greenleaf Whittier, *At Sundown* (Boston, 1893).

7. Stedman and Gould, II, 316.

8. *Poets of America*, p. 417.

9. Monroe, *A Poet's Life*, pp. 90–91.

10. Hamlin Garland, *Roadside Meetings* (New York, 1930), p. 336.

11. Monroe, *A Poet's Life*, p. 91.

12. Ibid., p. 84; p. 91.

13. Garland, *Roadside Meetings*, p. 337.

14. Stedman and Gould, II, 390. The letter is dated September 17, 1903.

15. Ibid., p. 340.

16. Lizette Reese, *A Victorian Village* (New York, 1929), p. 296.

17. Letter, Reese to Stedman, March 5, 1888. This letter is owned by Columbia University and is quoted by permission of the University.

18. Reese, p. 246.

19. William Sharp, *American Sonnets* (London, 1889).

20. Reese is responding to Stedman's most recent "note (enclosing one from Houghton & Co.). . . ." This letter is owned by Columbia University and is quoted by permission of the university.

21. Reese, pp. 246–47.

22. Letter, Reese to Stedman, April 7, 1899. This letter is owned by Columbia University and is quoted with permission of the university.

23. This comment is included in Stedman's brief biographical sketch. Only "in some cases, chiefly those of the most recent poets," did he add such comments. Otherwise, the notes are limited to "succinct biographical data." *An American Anthology*, pp. 777; 818.

24. *An American Anthology*, p. xxviii.

25. Gregory and Zaturenska, p. 83.

26. Percy MacKaye, "Introduction," in William Vaughn Moody, *Letters to Harriet* (Boston, 1935), p. 38.

27. Ibid., p. 39.

28. Stedman and Gould, I, 588.

29. Ibid., p. 589.

30. Ibid., pp. 593–94.

31. *The Century Magazine*, 76 (May 1908), 18–26.

32. MacKaye, p. 56.

33. Ibid., p. 39.

Chapter Eight

1. Letter, Stedman to O'Connor, 1880. This letter is owned by Columbia University and is published with the permission of the university.

2. Jones, "Introduction," *American Prose Masters*, pp. ix, x.

3. George J. Becker, *Documents of Modern Literary Realism* (Princeton, 1963), p. 105.

4. Joel Porte, Review of Edwin Fussel's *Lucifer in Harness, American Literature* 46 (November 1974), 405.

5. *Literary History of the United States:* History, p. vii.

6. Stedman and Gould, II, 129.

Selected Bibliography

PRIMARY SOURCES

I. Separate Works
The Prince's Ball. New York: Rudd & Carelton, 1860.
Poems, Lyrical and Idyllic. New York: Charles Scribner, 1860.
The Battle of Bull Run. New York: Rudd & Carelton, 1861.
Alice of Monmouth: An Idyl of the Great War, with Other Poems. New York: Rudd & Carelton, 1863.
The Blameless Prince and Other Poems. Boston: Fields, Osgood and Co., 1869.
The Poetical Works of Edmund Clarence Stedman. Boston: James R. Osgood and Co., 1873.
Victorian Poets. Boston: James R. Osgood and Co., 1875.
Victorian Poets, 13th ed. Rev. Boston: Houghton, Mifflin and Co., 1887.
Octavius Brooks Frothingham and the New Faith. New York: G. P. Putnam's Sons, 1876.
Hawthorne and Other Poems. Boston: James R. Osgood and Co., 1877.
Lyrics and Idylls with Other Poems. London: C. Kegan Paul & Co., 1879.
The Poetical Works of Edmund Clarence Stedman. Boston: Houghton Mifflin and Co., 1884.
Poets of America. Boston: Houghton Mifflin and Co., 1885.
The Nature and Elements of Poetry. Boston: Houghton Mifflin and Co., 1892.
Poems Now First Collected. Boston: Houghton Mifflin and Co., 1897.
The Poems of Edmund Clarence Stedman. Boston: Houghton, Mifflin, and Co., 1908.
Genius and Other Essays. New York: Moffat, Yard and Co., 1911.

II. Works Edited by Stedman
Cameos: Selected from the Works of Landor (with Thomas Bailey Aldrich). Boston: James R. Osgood and Co., 1873.
Osgood's Pocket Guide to Europe. Boston: James R. Osgood and Co., 1882.
A Library of American Literature (with Ellen Mackay Hutchinson). New York: C. L. Webster & Co., 1888–1890. 11 vols.
The Works of Edgar Allan Poe (with George E. Woodberry). Chicago: Stone & Kimball, 1894–1895. 10 vols.
An American Anthology, 1787–1900. Boston: Houghton Mifflin and Co., 1900.

The New York Stock Exchange. New York: New York Stock Exchange Historical Co., 1905.

SECONDARY SOURCES

The only book length study is STEDMAN, LAURA and GOULD, GEORGE M., *The Life and Letters of Edmund Clarence Stedman.* 2 vols. New York: Moffat, Yard and Co., 1910. An autobiographic biography, this essential work contains important letters by and to Stedman, portions of his uncompleted "Reminiscences," and excerpts from his works. Included in the second volume is a complete primary bibliography by Alice Marsland.

ALLEN, GAY W. *American Prosody.* New York: American Book Co., 1935. Contains a short discussion of Stedman's versification.

CARY, RICHARD. "The Genteel Tradition in America, 1850–1875." Ph.D. dissertation, Cornell University, 1952. A broad exposition of the limitations of Taylor, Stoddard, Stedman, and Aldrich. Valuable for its inclusion of 155 unpublished letters to and from Taylor and the other three.

———. *The Genteel Circle.* Ithaca: Cornell University Press, 1952. A short version of the above.

CONNER, FREDERICK W. *Cosmic Optimism: A study of the Interpretation of Evolution by American Poets from Emerson to Robinson.* Gainesville: University of Florida Press, 1949. Places Stedman's poetry and theoretical criticism within the context of a broad intellectual movement that influenced him greatly and to which he contributed.

DEMILLE, GEORGE. "Stedman, Arbiter of the Eighties." *PMLA,* XLI (September 1926), 756–66. Reprinted in *Literary Criticism in America.* New York: L. Mac Vegh, The Dial Press, 1931. An important and influential essay. While Stedman "has many of the qualities of a great critic," he can not, finally, be ranked with the greatest critics.

DODD, ANNA BOWMAN. "Edmund C. Stedman in New York and at Kelp Rock." *The Critic,* 7 (November 14, 1885), 229–31. A sympathetic and vivid picture of Stedman at home among his books and friends, by a close friend.

FULLER, MARGARET. *A New England Childhood.* Boston: Little, Brown and Co., 1916. Sensitive biographical study of Stedman's Norwich boyhood.

GOSSE, EDMUND W. *Transatlantic Dialogue: Selected American Correspondence.* Eds. Paul F. Mattheisen and Michael Millgate. Austin: University of Texas, 1965. Includes previously unpublished letters to and from Stedman and Gosse and a helpful introduction on transatlantic literary relations.

HIGGINSON, THOMAS W. *Carlyle's Laugh.* Boston: Houghton Mifflin and Co., 1909. Contains biographical-critical study of Stedman's

strengths and weaknesses by a distant relative and long-time friend.
HOWELLS, WILLIAM DEAN. "Editor's Easy Chair." *Harper's Monthly*, LXXXI (February 1911), 471–74. Moving tribute in the form of a review of *Life and Letters* by one of Stedman's oldest friends and sometime literary antagonist.

JONES, HOWARD MUMFORD. "Introduction." In William Cary Brownell, *American Prose Masters*. Cambridge, Mass.: The Belknap Press of Harvard University Press, 1967. An excellent brief assessment of the achievements of the genteel critics.

MACDONOUGH, A.R. "Edmund Clarence Stedman." *Scribner's Monthly*, 7 (November 18, 1873), 56–62. Early, encomiastic criticism in the magazine which was then carrying *Victorian Poets.*

MACKAYE, PERCY. "Introduction." In William Vaughn Moody, *Letters to Harriet*. Boston: Houghton Mifflin & Co., 1935. Includes sympathetic portrait of Stedman as "Nestor" to aspiring poets.

MILLER, RALPH N. "Associationist Psychology and Stedman's Theory of Poetry." *Markham Review* 5 (Summer 1976), 65–71. Explains "the key term" in Stedman's aesthetic theory, ideality, in the context of associationist psychology.

MOODY, WILLIAM VAUGHN. "Our Two Most Honored Poets." *Atlantic Monthly*, LXXXI (January 1898), 136–39. Review of work by Aldrich and Stedman's *Poems, Now First Collected.* "We feel something like reverence for a man who, in conditions which make for contentment and acquiescence, has not been able to escape [the] large afflictions" of the age.

PIATT, J. J. "Mr. Stedman's Poetry." *Atlantic Monthly*, XLI (March 1878) 313–19. A generous estimate of Stedman's position.

PRITCHARD, JOHN PAUL. *Criticism in America*. Norman: University of Oklahoma Press, 1956. More intelligent and sympathetic than the unfortunate chapter subtitle, "Lowell's Epigoni," would indicate.

SCHOLNICK, ROBERT J. "Whitman and the Magazines: Some Documentary Evidence." *American Literature*, 44 (May 1972), 222–46. Reports on Stedman's successful attempt to determine Whitman's standing with the major monthlies.

———— "The Shadowed Years: Mrs. Richards, Mr. Stedman, and Robinson." *Colby Library Quarterly*, 9 (June 1972), 510–31. Through new letters, shows just how much the help of Stedman meant to the best poet of his generation.

THORP, WILLARD. "Defenders of Ideality." In *Literary History of the United States*, ed. Robert E. Spiller, et. al. 3rd ed. rev. New York: Macmillan, 1963, pp. 809–826.

THORP, WILLARD. "Defenders of Ideality." In *Literary History of the United States*, ed. Robert E. Spiller et al. 3rd ed. rev. pp. 809–826. New York: Macmillan, 1948. Despite a reductive thesis, this essay does contain some useful insights into Stedman and his close associates.

Index